KU-010-145

THE GUIDE FOR WORKING FAMILIES

The Centre for Economic & Social Inclusion

This book has been produced by the Centre for Economic and Social Inclusion, an independent not for profit organisation dedicated to tackling disadvantage and promoting social justice. *Inclusion* offers research and policy services, tailored consultancy, bespoke and in-house training and runs a wide range of conferences and events.

Inclusion also produces the *Welfare to Work Handbook, Working in the UK: Newcomer's Handbook* and *The Young Person's Handbook*. More information about these publications, and our other products and services, is available on our website: www.cesi.org.uk

THE GUIDE FOR WORKING FAMILIES

By Dr Sarah Jenkins
IBSN: 1-870563-75-1
© 2006 Centre for Economic and Social Inclusion

Published 2006 by:
Centre for Economic and Social Inclusion
3rd floor, 89 Albert Embankment, London SE1 7TP

All rights reserved. Paragraphs from this book may be quoted, and short extracts reproduced without permission, with an appropriate credit, without prior permission. Full page reproduction, copying or transmission may be undertaken only with written permission or in accordance with the Copyright, Designs and Patents Act 1988.

Design: www.origin8creative.co.uk
Printing: www.cpd-group.co.uk

Disclaimer
Every effort has been taken to establish the accuracy of the advice in this handbook. However, we cannot guarantee the information contained is absolutely accurate. This is because guidance is constantly changing. Furthermore, partners can only endorse the contents of their own chapter(s). As far as the authors are aware, all chapters contain correct information at the time of writing.

THE AUTHOR

Dr Sarah Jenkins is an expert in the field of parents and work. During her career, she has spent many hours listening to parents talk of the difficulties and dilemmas they face when trying to combine their working career with a family life. She found that often parents were not aware of the support that is available to them and this became the motivation for writing this book.

Dr Jenkins has previously worked in academia and as an advisor to Government. She is now a consultant specialising in gender and work issues.

Other titles she has written include an academic book entitled *Gender, Place and the Labour Market* (2004, Ashgate), which explores the geography of women's participation in the labour market and discusses the factors that influence women's work/life balance and their decision-making processes.

ACKNOWLEDGMENTS

This guide has come together with the support of many people. The Centre for Economic and Social Inclusion would like to thank the following organisations for their involvement in helping us produce and check the relevant sections in this edition of *The Guide for Working Families*:

Department for Education and Skills

Department of Trade and Industry

The Department for Work and Pensions

The Equal Opportunities Commission

HM Revenue and Customs

Learning and Skills Council

One Parent Families

Women Returner's Network

A number of staff at the Centre for Economic and Social Inclusion have contributed to sections of this book:

Emmilie Aveling
Laurence Bell
Bee Brooke
Alex Doyle
Kelsey Froehlich
Kate Lawless
Louise Thomas
Zarita Westmore
Naeem Yar

Thanks are also due to Navida Jiwani for project managing the book's production.

THE GUIDE FOR WORKING FAMILIES

About this book   **5**

List of useful forms   **9**

List of abbreviations   **11**

Section one: Employment Rights   **13**

Introduction   14

1 Maternity Leave and Pay   16

2 Paternity Leave and Pay   36

3 Adoption Leave and Pay   46

4 Parental Leave   57

5 Working Flexibly and What to do if your child is ill   64

6 Breastfeeding at Work   76

Section two: Childcare Options 79

Introduction 80

7 Choosing Childcare: General Guidelines 81

8 Childcare in Your Home 89

9 Out-of-Home Childcare 100

10 Childcare for Disabled Children and Those with Special Educational Needs 127

Section three: Financial Support for Working Families 137

Introduction 138

11 Tax Credits 139

12 Child Benefit 149

13 Income Support and Other Benefits 155

14 Childcare Vouchers 161

15 Child Trust Fund 166

16 Sure Start Maternity Grant 177

17 Salary Sacrifice Scheme 181

18 Guardian's Allowance 188

19 The Enterprise Nursery Scheme 191

Section four: Returning to Education or Training 195

Introduction 196

20 Confidence-Building 198

21 Taking the First Steps 204

22 Learning and Qualifications 209

23 Financial Support for Learning 217

24 Organisations to Help You Return to Education 225

25 New Deals 230

Useful organisations 235

ABOUT THIS BOOK

Welcome to *The Guide for Working Families*. This book is designed to provide all the information you need to help you combine your working life with your family responsibilities.

The book is set out in the following 4 sections:

one   Employment Rights
two   Childcare Options
three Financial Support for Working Families
four   Returning to Education or Training

one. Employment Rights

This section outlines all the rights and responsibilities you have while working as a parent. It covers from the moment you or your partner discover that you are going to be a parent, through to working while caring for children. It includes your rights to time off work, what and when you must tell your employer that you want time off, and what payment you should receive during this time. This section also tells you how you can negotiate working flexibly to meet the needs of your family life.

two. Childcare Options

This section sets out the options you have when choosing childcare. It explains the difference between registered and non-registered childcare and the options available if you want to have childcare either in your home or out of your home. This chapter helps you to locate suitable childcare in your area, and suggests questions you may wish to ask a potential provider.

three.   Financial Support for Working Families

This section outlines the various different benefits and additional incomes you may qualify for. In this book it is not possible to cover all the government benefits that you may be able to apply for, but you will find the main ones that apply to working families. This includes direct benefits to top up your income, in addition to ways in which you may be able to benefit from tax relief or exemptions from National Insurance. It is important to remember that the figures quoted in this book were correct at the time of going to print for the financial year 2006 to 2007. Each chapter tells you where you are able to get the updated figures after this time.

four.   Returning to Education or Training

If you have had time off work to bring up your children and wish to return to work, this section outlines how you can update your skills or retrain for a new career. This includes what formal qualifications are available, and the benefits of gaining them. Many parents who have had time away from work doubt their ability to be able to return to work. This section includes a chapter on how to think about what skills you have to offer and building your confidence to return to work.

OUR WEBSITE

Throughout this book, we tell you about the different forms you need to fill in to apply for some of the rights and benefits you may be entitled to. We tell you where you can get the different forms from. In addition, where possible, we have put all the latest forms that you need in one place on our website for you to fill in. You can access these forms on **the website accompanying this book at www.theguideforworkingfamilies.org.uk**

A FEW HELPFUL DEFINITIONS

Who qualifies as a "partner"?

A partner is someone who lives with the parent and the child in an enduring family relationship but is not an immediate relative. This may include a male or female in a same-sex relationship. There is no minimum requirement for the length of time you need to be in the relationship to be classed as a partner. For more information on who qualifies as a partner, see page 37.

What is a civil partnership?

Two people of the same sex can form a civil partnership by signing a registration document. It provides same-sex couples with the same treatment in a wide range of legal matters as opposite-sex couples who enter into a civil marriage.

Partners who are in same-sex relationships are entitled to receive the same maternity, paternity, parental and adoption leave as heterosexual couples.

Who are dependant children?

A dependant child is classified as someone who is:

- under the age of 16, or
- under the age of 19 and studying for A-levels, GNVQ level 3 or equivalent, and
  studying for more than 12 hours a week at school or college (not including homework, private study, unsupervised study or meal breaks)

A child stops being a dependant when they:

- are 16 and over and work for 24 hours or more a week
- get married
- get certain benefits in their own right (for example Income Support, income-based Jobseeker's Allowance, Incapacity Benefit) ·
- are on a training course and getting a particular training allowance
- have employed trainee status
- are in custody
- are in care for more than 8 weeks (unless they come home for at least 2 nights a week)

What is parental responsibility?

Having parental responsibility means that you have the right to make important decisions about your child's life in areas such as medical treatment and education. It also means that you have a duty to care for and protect the child.

Who has parental responsibility?

If the parents of a child are married to each other or if they have jointly adopted a child, then they both have parental responsibility. This is not automatically the case for unmarried parents. The following are a few points to consider:

- a mother always has parental responsibility for her child
- a father has parental responsibility only if he is married to the mother or has acquired legal responsibility for his child
- living with the mother, even for a long time, does not automatically give a father parental responsibility
- parental responsibility does not always pass to the natural father if the mother dies and the parents were not married
- parental responsibility does not mean paying maintenance or child support – the two things are not connected

If you are unsure about whether or not you have parental responsibility, visit www.direct.gov.uk for more advice and guidance.

LIST OF FORMS AND INFORMATION AVAILABLE ON OUR WEBSITE

www.theguideforworkingfamilies.org.uk

one. Employment Rights

Maternity Leave and Pay

Form type	Document
Model letter	Employer to acknowledge maternity leave
SMP1	Why I cannot pay you SMP
E15	Pay and time off work for parents of babies due or born on or after 6 April 2003

Paternity Leave and Pay

Form type	Document
SC3	Statutory Paternity Leave and Pay
SPP1	"I cannot pay you Statutory Paternity Pay (SPP)"

Adoption Leave and Pay

Form type	Document
SC4	Self Certificate Adoption Paternity
Model letter	Employer response to request for leave or pay
	Adoptive Parents: rights to leave and pay when a child is adopted from overseas (produced by DTI)
PL518	Adoptive Parents: Rights to leave and pay when a child is placed for adoption within the UK
PL517	Working fathers: Rights to Paternity Leave and Pay
E16	Pay and time off work for adoptive parents
	Matching certificate adoptive parents leave and pay

Breastfeeding at work

Form type	Document
HSE	Guide for New and Expectant Mothers

Working flexibly

Form type	Document
FW(A)	Flexible Working Application Form
FW(B)	Flexible Working Application Acceptance Form
FW(C)	Flexible Working Application Rejection Form
FW(D)	Flexible Working Appeal Form
FW(E)	Flexible Working Appeal Reply Form
FW(F)	Flexible Working Extension of Time Limit Form
FW(G)	Flexible Working Notice of Withdrawal Form
PL520	Guidance on your right to request flexible working – DTI
ET1	Employment Tribunal application form

two. Childcare

Out of home childcare

Form type	Document
NCMA	Guide to choosing the right childcare

Disabled and SEN children

Form type	Document
SEN	"Special Educational Needs – A Guide for Parents and Carers."
	Working Families Fact sheet 12: Childcare for Children with Disabilities

three. Financial Support for Working Families

Child Benefit

Form type	Document
	Child Benefit claim form
	Child Benefit claiming notes
	Child Benefit appeal form

Sure Start Maternity Grant

Form type	Document
SF100	Maternity Grant claim form

Guardian's Allowance

Form type	Document
bg1	Guardian's Allowance claim form
bg1	Guardian's Allowance notes

ABBREVIATIONS

Abbreviation	Full name
AA	Attendance Allowance
ACAS	Advisory, Conciliation and Arbitration Service
ACL	Adult and Community Learning
ALG	Adult Learning Grant
ALM	Additional Maternity Leave
BTEC	Business and Technology Education Council
CA	Carer's Allowance
CB	Child Benefit
CDL	Career Development Loans
CIS	Children's Information Service
CTC	Child Tax Credit
CTF	Child Trust Fund
DFES	Department for Education and Skills
DLA	Disability Living Allowance
DTI	Department of Trade and Industry
DWP	Department for Work and Pensions
EI	External Institution
EMA	Education Maintenance Allowance
EU	European Union
FE	Further Education
HEI	Higher Education Institution
HMRC	Her Majesty's Revenue and Customs
IAPA	International Au Pair Association
IB	Incapacity Benefit
IS	Income Support
ISCIS	Independent Schools Council Information Service

LEA	Local Education Authority
MA	Maternity Allowance
MP	Member of Parliament
MPP	Maternity Pay Period
NCMA	National Childminding Association
NDLP	New Deal for Lone Parents
NI	National Insurance
NICs	National Insurance Contributions
NICMA	Northern Ireland Childminding Association
NVQ	National Vocational Qualification
OML	Ordinary Maternity Leave
PANN	Professional Association of Nursery Nurses
QCA	Qualifications and Curriculum Authority
REC	Recruitment and Employment Confederation
SAP	Statutory Adoption Pay
SEN	Special Educational Needs
SENCO	Special Educational Needs Co-ordinator
SMP	Statutory Maternity Pay
SPP	Statutory Paternity Pay
SSP	Statutory Sick Pay
TIGER	Tailored Interaction Guidance on Employment Rights
UCAS	University and Colleges Admissions Service
WBL	Work-based Learning
WRN	Women Returners' Network
WTC	Working Tax Credit

EMPLOYMENT RIGHTS

section
one

INTRODUCTION TO EMPLOYMENT RIGHTS

section **one**

Are you working and have just discovered that you are about to become a family? In order to ensure that you have the option to use all the leave and pay that may be available to you, this section will help you find out:

- what you need to tell your employer
- when you need to tell them
- how much time off you are entitled to
- how much you will be paid during your time off

If you are the mother of the child, the **Maternity Leave and Pay** chapter (see page 16) tells you when you must inform your employer that you are pregnant. This chapter also helps you find out if you qualify for up to 12 months' maternity leave, and what you will be paid during this time.

If you are the father or partner, you may be entitled to paid time off from work to support the mother and your newborn child. The **Paternity Leave and Pay** chapter (see page 37) will help you to find out if you qualify for leave and how much you will be paid during this time.

If you and/or your partner are adopting a child, you may be entitled to paid leave. The **Adoption Leave and Pay** chapter (see page 46) helps you establish if you qualify for this and how much you may be paid during this time.

When you have young children you may want to take time off work to spend time with them. If you have a child under 6 years old, you may be entitled to take **Parental Leave** (see page 57) to be with them through potentially difficult times, such as settling them into a new school or during the introduction of new childcare arrangements. This chapter will help you work out if you qualify for this.

If, when you return to work, you wish to continue breastfeeding, your employer must be aware of your needs. The **Breastfeeding at Work** chapter (see page 76) explains the responsibilities that you and your employer must be aware of to set up this option.

Once you have had your child, regardless of how much planning and preparation you have done, you may need more flexibility at your place of work. The **Working Flexibly** chapter (see page 64) outlines the various options that may be available to help you combine work and your new family life. If you are pregnant and wanting to return to work after the baby is born, it is a good idea to talk through some of the suggested options with your employer to prepare for when you return to work. This chapter also outlines some of the options you may have **when your child is ill**.

MATERNITY LEAVE AND PAY

This chapter outlines what maternity leave and pay you are entitled to if you are working while you are pregnant.

1

1 MATERNITY LEAVE AND PAY

All maternity rights apply to full-time and part-time employees no matter how many hours are worked. However, the length of time you have been employed by your employer may affect your entitlements.

KEY FACTS

- Ordinary Maternity Leave is paid for 6 months.
- If you qualify, your first 6 weeks of Maternity Leave is paid at 90% of your regular earnings.
- Further maternity pay is £108.85 a week if you qualify, this increases to 9 months if your expected birth is on or after 1 April 2007.
- If you qualify, an extra 6 months' unpaid Additional Maternity Leave is optional.
- At the end of your maternity leave you are entitled to return to the same job as before. If that is not reasonably practicable, you should be offered a similar job on terms and conditions that are not less favourable than your original job.

TELLING YOUR EMPLOYER YOU ARE PREGNANT

When should I tell my employer?

You must tell your employer no later than the end of your 25th week of pregnancy. This is the latest you must tell your employer that you are pregnant, however, you should consider telling them sooner. As soon as your employer is aware that you are pregnant, they will conduct a health and safety assessment for you (see below), and you can have time off work for medical appointments (see page 20).

You must inform them:

- that you are pregnant
- when you are due to give birth – you are required to show your employer a medical certificate (this would normally be a maternity certificate (Form MAT B1), which you get from your GP or midwife; your employer cannot start paying you Statutory Maternity Pay until they have the certificate.)
- when you intend your maternity leave to start – your employer has the right to ask you to put this in writing

Employers' responsibilities

Employers must notify the employee of the date that her maternity leave will finish within 28 days of receiving notification of her pregnancy. The Department of Trade and Industry has created a model letter for doing this, which can be found on the website accompanying this book.

An employee cannot normally start her maternity leave unless she has given her employer the required notice, except in the following circumstances:

- if the employee gives birth before the date she has notified. In which case the maternity leave automatically starts on the day after birth

- if the employee is absent from work due to a pregnancy-related reason after the beginning of week 36 of her pregnancy, but before the date she has notified as the start of her leave. In this case, her maternity leave automatically begins on the second day of her absence

HEALTH AND SAFETY RISK ASSESSMENT

Once you have told your employer that you are pregnant, your employer must undertake a risk assessment to ensure that the tasks that you carry out at work are not going to be damaging to you or your baby. Your employer has a right to request a certificate from a GP or midwife confirming your pregnancy (Form Mat B1).

Risk assessments should generally include consideration of the risks for those who are pregnant, those who have given birth or miscarried in the last 6 months, and those who are breastfeeding.

Employers

By law, you are required to assess the risks to all your employees and to do what is reasonably practicable to control these risks. You are also required to take into account risks to new and expectant mothers while assessing risks into your work activity. If a risk cannot be avoided, you are required to make changes to the working conditions or hours of a new or expectant mother, offer her alternative work, or if that is not possible, suspend her for as long as possible to protect her health and safety and that of her baby.

THE ASSESSMENT

Step 1. A risk assessment must be conducted to find out if any of your working conditions could jeopardise the health and safety of you or your baby. This will include a consideration of whether you are likely to experience any of the following at work:

• shocks or vibrations	• excess heat or cold
• work in confined spaces	• high pressure
• chemical or biological agents	• manual handling
• constant sitting	• passive smoking
• continuous standing	• stress
• excess travelling	• work at heights

Step 2. If a significant risk is found, your employer must do all that they can to remove it or prevent exposure to it.

Step 3. Your employer should give you information on the risk and what action has been taken.

Step 4. If any risk remains, your employer should temporarily alter your working conditions or hours of work if it is reasonably practicable to do so.

Step 5. If the risk cannot be avoided, you employer may offer you suitable alternative employment on terms and conditions that are not less than your original job. In deciding whether an offer is suitable, consideration should be given to working conditions, status, hours of work, location, travelling time and pay.

Step 6. If there is no suitable employment available, your employer may suspend you on full pay for as long as is necessary to avoid the risk. You should be paid the same during this time as you would if you were working normally.

For more information on risk assessments, contact the Equal Opportunities Commission (see page 247 for their contact details).

TIME OFF FROM WORK FOR ANTENATAL CARE

Key Facts

- All pregnant employees are entitled to time off for antenatal care.
- All time off for antenatal care must be paid at your normal rate of pay.
- Antenatal care may include relaxation and parentcraft classes, as well as medical examinations.
- All rights apply regardless of how long you have worked for your employer.

Can I have time off work to attend antenatal classes?

Yes. You are entitled to time off to keep appointments for antenatal care. This can include relaxation classes and parentcraft classes as long as these are on the advice of your GP, midwife or registered health visitor.

Do I need to prove I have an appointment?

Except in the case of your first appointment, you must be prepared to provide both:

- a certificate confirming you are pregnant (this is usually Form MAT B1, which you can get from your GP or midwife)
- an appointment card showing that an appointment has been made

Will I lose money if I have time off?

No. You should be paid at your normal wage during your time off. If your working hours vary from week to week, your employer should work out the average hours you have worked over the last 12 complete working weeks.

Employers

It is illegal for you to dismiss an employee, or select her for redundancy in preference to other comparable employees, solely or mainly because she has sought time off for antenatal care.

MATERNITY LEAVE

Compulsory Maternity Leave and Ordinary Maternity Leave are available to all mothers. You may also qualify for optional Additional Maternity Leave. Remember:

- to take advantage of any maternity leave you must give your employer proper notice (see "Telling your employer you are pregnant", page 17)

Compulsory Maternity Leave

You cannot return to work immediately after giving birth because Compulsory Maternity Leave lasts until:

- 2 weeks from giving birth or
- 4 weeks from giving birth if you work in a factory or
- a later date if there is a health and safety reason that stops you from working – your employer will inform you if this is the case

Ordinary Maternity Leave

All pregnant employees are entitled to 26 weeks' (6 months') Ordinary Maternity Leave. This applies regardless of how long you have been working for your employer.

Additional Maternity Leave

Key Facts

- If you have worked for your employer for 26 continuous weeks by the time you are 26 weeks pregnant, you are entitled to an extra 26 weeks Additional Maternity Leave (AML). This means that you can have a total of 1 year at home with your child.

- AML begins at the end of Ordinary Maternity Leave.

- AML is usually unpaid.

- AML is optional. You must inform your employer if you do not wish to take it.

- From April 2007, the qualifying service of 26 weeks for AML is being removed. All women will therefore have the option of up to one year's maternity leave.

When can I start my Maternity Leave?

You can start your Maternity Leave any time after week 29 of your pregnancy.

To help you plan your maternity leave, you can use the Government's interactive website at www.direct.gov.uk/Employment/Employees

What happens if my baby dies?

You are entitled to full Maternity Leave if your baby is stillborn after 24 weeks of pregnancy.

If the baby is born alive at any point in the pregnancy, but dies later, you are entitled to paid Maternity Leave in the usual way.

Do I still get my employee benefits when I am on Maternity Leave?

Yes, you remain an employee throughout your OML and are entitled to receive all your contractual benefits except your wages, for example, if you are entitled to a staff discount on particular products, you should continue to receive this discount while on Maternity Leave. This also applies to all other benefits such as the use of a company car or mobile phone, professional subscriptions, participation in share schemes or health club membership.

However, this does not apply while you are on Additional Maternity Leave.

Will I still get annual leave while on Maternity Leave?

If you are entitled to paid holiday where you work, then you should also get the same holiday entitlement while on Maternity Leave. This entitlement includes:

- during OML, you will accumulate the same amount of holidays you would normally be entitled to
- during AML, you will accumulate annual holidays on the basis of 4 weeks per year

Your annual holidays must be used within the year in which they were awarded. You cannot automatically carry them over into a new year.

If you wish to take your annual holiday at the end of your maternity leave, it is advisable that you discuss this with your employer before you begin your maternity leave.

Does being on Maternity Leave affect my pension?

Being on Maternity Leave does not affect your working record, for example, when your redundancy payments, pension rights or pay increments are being calculated.

While you are receiving Maternity Pay, you continue to benefit from any pension contributions made by your employer. If your company scheme requires you to contribute, your contribution should be worked out on the amount of Maternity Pay you are receiving. If you decide to take unpaid Additional Maternity Leave (AML) you cannot receive pension contributions during the time you are on unpaid leave.

From 1 April 2007, you can be paid for up to 3 months of AML and you continue to receive pension contributions for the period you are receiving Maternity Pay.

MORE TIME OFF WITH YOUR CHILD

If you would like to organise additional time off with your child, then you may also qualify for:

- Parental Leave (see chapter 4)
- Flexible working hours (see chapter 5)

MATERNITY PAY AND ALLOWANCE

While you are on Maternity Leave, you may be entitled to receive Maternity Pay and Maternity Allowance. Follow the flow diagram opposite to find out if you qualify for Statutory Maternity Pay or Maternity Allowance.

STATUTORY MATERNITY PAY

Statutory Maternity Pay is:

- a weekly payment paid to you by your employer when you stop work to have your baby
- paid for 26 weeks (6 months) and this is called the Maternity Pay Period (MPP)
- the government is extending SMP from 26 to 39 weeks (6 to 9 months) and this will apply to you if your expected birth date is on or after 1 April 2007
- not subject to tax or National Insurance

I'M PREGNANT AND WORKING –
WHAT TYPE OF MATERNITY PAY AM I ENTITLED TO?

Are you SELF-EMPLOYED or have you been employed in your current job LESS THAN 26 WEEKS by the 26th week of your pregnancy?

NO

YES

If ALL 3 of the following statements apply to you:

- your average weekly earnings during weeks 18-26 of your pregnancy are equal or more than £84
- you did/will give your employer at least 28 days' notice of the day you wish your maternity leave to start
- you did/will leave work after the 30th week of pregnancy

NO

YES

You may be entitled to receive **MATERNITY ALLOWANCE** for 26 weeks

You are entitled to receive **STATUTORY MATERNITY PAY** for 26 weeks

YES

Are you earnings on average at least £30 a week?

NO

Sorry, you are not entitled to any maternity pay

To check if you qualify for Statutory Maternity Pay, answer the following questions:

	YES	No
Have you been employed by your employer for a continuous period of at least 26 weeks before you are 26 weeks pregnant?		
Are your average earnings between weeks 18 and 26 of pregnancy equal to or more than £84 a week?		
Did you give your employer at least 28 days' notice of the date you wish your SMP to start? (You can change your maternity leave dates, as long as you give your employer 28 days' notice.)		
Will you be starting your maternity leave any time after week 30 of your pregnancy?		
Did you give your employer medical evidence of the date your baby is due (Form MAT B1 – see page 18)		

If you answered yes to all of the questions above, you qualify for SMP. If you answered no to any questions, you may still qualify for Maternity Allowance (see page 28).

How much is Statutory Maternity Pay?

- For the first 6 weeks, SMP is 90% of your average weekly earnings
- For the remaining 20 weeks, SMP is either £108.85 or 90% of your average weekly earnings, whichever is the lowest
- Some employers may provide additional maternity pay to top up your SMP. For example, some employers may offer you full pay during your maternity leave. In exchange, they may ask you to agree to work a minimum period upon your return, for example one or two years. You will need to ask your employer if this is applies to you. This would not affect your SMP
- For women expecting babies on or after 1 April 2007, SMP is being extended from 26 to 39 weeks (6 to 9 months)

Employers

You are reimbursed 92% of the SMP or 104.5% if your total National Insurance (NI) liability in the previous tax year was no more than £45,000 (small employers).

You can deduct from your next payment of PAYE and NI contributions, student loan and construction industry payments to HM Revenue and Customs an amount equal to 92% of the SMP you have paid out in the preceding period. Small employers can deduct 100% of the SMP they have paid out, plus 4.5% for the tax year 2006/7 in compensation for employers' NI costs.

If an employee does not qualify for SMP, you should give her Form SMP1 "Why I cannot pay you SMP". This form will explain to her why she does not qualify. This is available on the website accompanying this book, from Jobcentre Plus Offices or on the DWP website at www.dwp.gov.uk/resourcecentre or call them on 020 7712 2171.

You can get more information on SMP from the HMRC employer's help book E15 "Pay and time off work for parents for babies due or born on or after 6 April 2003". This is available on the website accompanying this book or from the Employers Orderline on 08457 646 646. Alternatively call the Employers Helpline on 08457 143 143 or visit www.hmrc.gov.uk/helpsheets/2006/e15.pdf

Do I have to return to work?

Once you qualify for SMP you will receive payment. This is regardless of whether you do not intend to return to work after maternity leave, or whether you left work before the SMP payments start. Also see page 32 on paying back your maternity pay.

What happens if my baby is born prematurely?

Your SMP may or may not be affected depending on how premature your baby is. If your baby is earlier than expected, but after you have started your Maternity Payment Period (MPP), your SMP is not affected. If your baby is born before your MPP, but after the qualifying week (see page 26), you must inform your employer within 3 weeks of giving birth. You will receive SMP for 26 weeks, starting the day following the birth of your baby.

What happens if I am off work for a pregnancy-related illness?

If you are absent from work, wholly or partly because of your pregnancy, this may trigger the start of your Maternity Pay Period (MPP). If you are absent from work for a pregnancy-related illness, on or after the 4th week before the baby is due, your MPP will start automatically on the 2nd complete day you are absent from work for a pregnancy related illness.

How is Statutory Maternity Pay paid?

It is usually paid in the same way and at the same time as your wages would be paid.

When will I start receiving Statutory Maternity Pay?

Your first payment will be the first Sunday after the last day you worked before starting your maternity leave.

If you are expecting your baby on or after 1 April 2007, SMP will begin the day you start your maternity leave.

Can I work and receive Statutory Maternity Pay?

No. SMP is calculated weekly. If you do any work for your employer during your MPP, you will not receive SMP for that week. If, after the birth, you do any work for an employer who did not employ you during the 26th week of your pregnancy, your SMP will stop completely.

Can I receive Statutory Maternity Pay if I do not live in the UK?

If you work for a UK employer overseas, you may qualify for SMP. For further information contact your local HMRC (Her Majesty's Revenue and Customs).

MATERNITY ALLOWANCE (MA)

If you do not qualify for Statutory Maternity Pay you may qualify for Maternity Allowance (MA).

Maternity Allowance is:

For women who work but who do not qualify for SMP (for example, the recently employed or the self-employed)

- paid by Jobcentre Plus
- not subject to tax or National Insurance
- paid for 26 weeks (6 months) – note, this is increasing to 39 weeks (9 months) for women expecting to give birth on or after 1 April 2007

To check if you qualify for Maternity Allowance, answer the following questions:

	YES	NO
Have you been employed and/or self-employed for at least 26 weeks in the test period? The test period is the 66 weeks up to and including the week before the week your baby is due.		
Have you earned on average at least £30 per week or more in any 13 weeks during the test period?		

If you answered yes to the questions above you qualify for MA.

How much is Maternity Allowance?

MA is paid for up to a maximum of 26 weeks. The amount you receive will either be £108.85 a week or 90% of your average weekly earnings – whichever is the lowest.

The government is extending MA from 26 to 39 weeks (6 to 9 months). This will apply to you if your expected delivery date is on or after 1 April 2007.

If you are receiving MA, you may also be able to receive Income Support. (see page 154)

How is Maternity Allowance paid?

MA is paid either weekly or every 4 weeks into an account. You can choose to have it paid:

- into a Post Office card account, or
- paid directly into your bank or building society account

Can I work and receive Maternity Allowance?

No. You will lose MA for each day that you work during your MA period.

Can I receive Maternity Allowance if I do not live in the UK?

If you qualify for MA, you may be able to receive it if you live abroad. Check this with your local Jobcentre Plus.

Will my Maternity Allowance be affected by other benefits?

Your MA may be reduced, or not paid at all, if you get other social security benefits or a training allowance (including an allowance under the Youth Training Scheme), see the box below.

The impact of receiving Maternity Allowance on other benefits

Jobseeker's Allowance (JSA) While you are receiving MA you will not be entitled to receive Jobseeker's Allowance.

Income Support (IS) You are still entitled to receive IS but the amount you get will be reduced by the amount of MA you receive. If you are receiving Child Tax Credit, you will more than likely not qualify for IS, as MA is more than the amount you are allowed to receive.

Working Tax Credit (WTC) If you were working and claiming WTC prior to becoming pregnant, you will continue to receive it during your maternity period. If you did not previously qualify for WTC, and this is your first baby, you may now qualify.

Housing Benefit (HB) If you were receiving HB prior to giving birth, you will continue to receive it while receiving MA.

Incapacity Benefit (IB) You will receive either IB or MA, whichever is the highest.

OTHER EMPLOYMENT RIGHTS WHILE ON MATERNITY LEAVE

No sick pay

You are entitled to sick leave but are not entitled to receive Statutory Sick Pay (SSP) while you are receiving maternity pay, either SMP or MA. This rule applies even if you return to work early and then fall ill before the planned 26 weeks is over. If this happens you will receive maternity pay (SMP or MA) not SSP.

Employers

An employee who is absent from work due to illness will normally be able to take sick leave until she starts Maternity Leave on the date notified to her employer. If the illness is unrelated to the pregnancy she can remain on sick leave and receive SSP right up to the date of the baby's birth, or until the date on which she intends to start her Maternity Leave.

However, if the illness is pregnancy-related, the Maternity Leave automatically starts on the second day of absence following week 36 of the pregnancy.

Where an employee is unable to attend work at the end of their Maternity Leave due to sickness, the normal contractual arrangements for SSP apply.

Dismissal or resignation

If you resign or are dismissed from your job before the date you have chosen to start your Maternity Leave, you lose the right to Maternity Leave.

If you are working up to and during week 26 of pregnancy, you will still qualify for SMP.

RETURNING TO WORK

Before starting your Maternity Leave, you will have been notified by your employer of the date you are due to return to work (see employers' responsibilities on page 18).

If you intend to return to work immediately after the end of your Maternity Leave, you do not have to give your employer advance notice.

If you intend to return to work before the end of your Maternity Leave, you must give your employer at least 28 days' notice of the date of your return.

If you qualify for Additional Maternity Leave, but do not wish to use it, you should give your employer 28 days' notice of your return (this changes to 8 weeks from April 2007). This is because you are returning to work before the end of your full Maternity Leave allowance.

Can I return to my old job?

When you return to work after Maternity Leave you are entitled to return to the same job, or one of a similar status, with the same terms and conditions as you had before you left. This is unless you have been made redundant.

What happens if I am made redundant?

Before your contract ends, you may be offered a suitable alternative vacancy. This can be with an associated employer or with a new company which may have taken over. The new contract must take immediate effect from the ending of your old one.

If the employer offers you a suitable alternative vacancy but you refuse it, you may give up your right to a redundancy payment.

Further information can be found in the Redundancy Payment booklet (PL 808) which can be found only on the DTI website at www.dti.gov.uk/employment/redundancy or call their helpline on 0845 145 0004.

Can I change my working hours when I return to work?

Parents with young children (under 6 years old, or under 18 if your child is disabled) have the right to request flexible working hours, see chapter 5 for more information.

What if I don't want to return to work?

If you do not wish to return to work after your Maternity Leave, you must give your employer the notification agreed in your contract.

I don't want to return to work, do I have to pay back my maternity pay?

Payment of SMP is not dependant upon your intention to return to work for your employer after your baby is born. If you qualify for SMP, you will get it, and keep it, even if you do not return to work. If you qualify for SML, then you can hand in your notice to your employers while on Maternity Leave and serve your agreed notice period without having to pay anything back. This means, for example, that if you have a 3-month notice period, you can hand in your resignation 3 months before your due return date. Then you do not have to return to work at all or repay any money. Statutory Maternity Pay is payable to you whatever you decide to do.

If you are receiving a top-up of maternity pay from your company (for example, some companies may pay the full wage for part or all of the Maternity Leave) then the amount of time that you must work for that employer after you return to work will be written in your employment contract. The rules determining the expected number of days you must work upon return from Maternity Leave are entirely determined by the individual employer. If you then fail to work these required days, however, remember that your company cannot reclaim all your money, you are allowed to keep the SMP, and you would only have to pay back the extra "top-up" money.

SUMMARY OF MATERNITY PAY

	TYPE OF MATERNITY PAY	
	Statutory Maternity Pay (SMP)	Maternity Allowance (MA)
How long does maternity pay last?	26 weeks OR 39 weeks if you expect your baby on or after 1 April 2007	26 weeks OR 39 weeks if you expect your baby on or after 1 April 2007
How much will I be paid?	First 6 weeks: 90% of your average weekly earnings Next 20 weeks: either £108.85 a week OR 90% of your average weekly earnings, whichever is lowest	Either £108.85 a week OR 90% of your average weekly earnings, whichever is lowest
How will I be paid?	The same way you are normally paid your wages	Either: 1 Directly into your bank/ building society account OR 2 A Post Office card account

	Statutory Maternity Pay (SMP)	Maternity Allowance (MA)
When is it paid?	Currently: it begins on the first Sunday after the last day you worked before Maternity Leave From April 2007: SMP will be paid from the day you start your Maternity Leave	Weekly or every 4 weeks
Who is it paid by?	Your employer	Jobcentre Plus
Am I able to work while receiving Maternity Pay?	If you do any work for your employer, you will lose your Maternity Pay for that week Note: this is going to change for women expecting babies on or after 1 April 2007 when you will be able to work for a limited number of days for your employer and still keep your SMP	No – you will lose MA for every day you work This is going to change for women expecting babies on or after 1 April 2007 when you will be able to work for a limited number of days and still keep your MA
Is it available to UK citizens *not* working in the UK?	Possibly: contact your HMRC Office for further information	It is possible – see www.dwp.gov.uk/advisers/ni17a/ under Maternity Allowance
Do I have to return to work if I receive Maternity Pay?	Once you have qualified for SMP, you will receive it even if you do not intend to return to work	No
Can I receive sick pay while receiving Maternity Pay?	No – even if you have returned to work before SMP ends, if you fall sick you will receive SMP not Statutory Sick Pay	No – even if you have returned to work before MA ends, if you fall sick you will receive MA not Statutory Sick Pay
If I am made redundant while on Maternity Leave, can I still receive Maternity Pay?	Yes	Not applicable

FURTHER INFORMATION

- For more details on SMP and MA, see leaflet NI 17A – A guide to Maternity Benefits, which is available on the DWP website www.dwp.gov.uk/advisers/ni17a; this form is also available on the website accompanying this book

- Both employers and employees can visit the DTI website at www.dti.gov.uk/er/workingparents.htm and its interactive guidance site Directgov www.direct.gov.uk/Employment/Employees to work out entitlements to Maternity Leave and Pay, alternatively, call them on 020 7215 5000

- Contact ACAS (Advisory, Conciliation and Arbitration Service) for advice on individual cases and up-to-date advice on employment relation issues; call them on 08457 474747 or visit their website at www.acas.org.uk

- Working Families provide a free legal helpline for low-income families – you can call them on 0800 013 0313 or visit the website at www.workingfamilies.org.uk

PATERNITY LEAVE AND PAY

Paternity rights have been established to enable fathers to support the mother, and also to enable him to have time to bond with their baby during those early days of family life.

2

2 PATERNITY LEAVE AND PAY

KEY FACTS

- Fathers are entitled to up to 2 weeks' paid Paternity Leave.
- Paternity Pay is £108.85 if you qualify.

Who qualifies as a "partner"?

A partner is someone who lives with the mother of the baby in a long-term relationship but is not a relative.

Please note that when we refer to "partners", this may include partners in a same sex couple. Where this chapter refers to employees as "father", "he", "him" or "his", this should be taken to include those female same-sex partners who qualify.

If you are the father of a child but do not live with the biological mother, you are still able to apply for Paternity Leave.

Members of the armed forces and office holders such as police officers, MPs, and the judiciary do not qualify for paternity leave.

If you are the partner of a mother adopting a child, please see chapter 3.

TIME OFF FOR ANTENATAL CARE

Fathers are not entitled to time off to accompany their partners to antenatal appointments.

PATERNITY LEAVE

Paternity rights apply to all employees, regardless of the hours you work, provided that you meet the qualifying conditions.

How much time off work can I have?

You can take up to two weeks' Paternity Leave. This time off must be taken in one go. It cannot be taken as odd days or as 2 separate weeks. So, you can take just 1 week or 2 continuous weeks' Paternity Leave.

How do I qualify for Paternity Leave?

You are eligible for Paternity Leave if you are, or expect to be, responsible for your baby's upbringing and are taking time off to support the mother or to care for the new baby, see page 8 on parental responsibility.

To qualify for Paternity Leave you must be able to say yes to A and B		
A		B
Are you the biological father of the baby?		Have you worked continuously for the same employer for 26 weeks by the 25th week of pregnancy and will continue to do so up to the birth of the child?
and/or	AND	
Are you the mother's husband, civil partner or partner?		

See also chart on page 41. Even if you do not qualify for Paternity Leave, you may still qualify for Statutory Paternity Pay, see page 43.

Will I qualify for Paternity Leave if the baby is stillborn or dies following the birth?

You are entitled to paid Paternity Leave if your baby is stillborn after 24 weeks of pregnancy.

If the baby is born alive at any point in the pregnancy but dies later, you are entitled to paid Paternity Leave in the usual way.

When do I have to tell my employer?

You must tell your employer that you intend to take Paternity Leave before the end of the 25th week of the pregnancy.

When can I take the leave?

Paternity Leave cannot be taken until the birth of the baby. Leave can start on any day of the week, as long as you have given the required notice.

You can choose to start your leave:

- on the date of the baby's birth (whether this is earlier or later than expected)
- on a chosen date as notified to your employer which falls after the first day of the expected birth date
- within 56 days of the actual birth of the child *or* if the child is born earlier than expected, between the birth and 56 days from the first day of the expected week of birth

If you are at work on the day you have specified your leave to start (for example, the expected date of the delivery) your leave will begin on the next day.

What if I have told my employer a specific date but the baby is not born yet?

You cannot take Paternity Leave or receive Statutory Paternity Pay (SPP) before the birth of the baby. If the baby isn't born by the date specified, then you must change the date.

Can I change my mind about when the leave starts?

You can change your mind about the date you wish your leave to start as long as you give your employer 28 days' notice. You cannot change the length of leave you want to take.

If the baby is born before it is due, you may not have been able to give the required notice period for leave and pay. In this case, you should give the information and declaration required on Form SC3 "Statutory Paternity Leave and Pay" as soon as is reasonably possible. This form is available on the website accompanying this book.

What should I do if I want to take Parental Leave immediately after Paternity Leave?

In addition to your Paternity Leave, you may be able to take additional leave, see chapter 4 on Parental Leave. You will need to give the required notice to your employer for both Paternity Leave and Parental Leave.

STATUTORY PATERNITY PAY

While you are on Paternity Leave, you may be entitled to receive Statutory Paternity Pay (SPP).

How much is it?

Statutory Paternity Pay is £108.85 a week or 90% of your average weekly earnings if this is less than £108.85.

How do I qualify for Statutory Paternity Pay (SPP)?

To qualify for SPP, you must tell your employer that you would like to be paid SPP at least 28 days beforehand.

You must have an average weekly earning of £84 or more. You do not have to pay National Insurance to qualify.

If you do not qualify for SPP because you are not earning more than £84 a week, you may be able to get other financial support while on Paternity Leave. Additional financial support may be available through Income Support, Housing Benefit, Council Tax Benefit, Tax Credits or a Sure Start Maternity Grant. Further information is available in section 3 of this book "Financial Support for Working Families", and from your local Jobcentre Plus office or Social Security office. To locate your nearest Jobcentre Plus, visit www.jobcentreplus.gov.uk or call DWP on 020 7712 2171.

If I change jobs before the baby is born will I still qualify for Paternity Leave and Pay?

Unless your new employer is an associated employer, you will probably not qualify. The document "Continuous employment and a week's pay" (PL 711) will tell you more about when time with a previous employer may

AM I ENTITLED TO PATERNITY LEAVE?

Regardless of the number of hours you work, if you are an employee who is, or expects to be, responsible for your baby's upbringing and are taking time off to support the mother or to care for the new baby, follow the questions below to find out if you can claim Paternity Leave.

Are you in the armed forces or do you hold a position in public office, such as in the police force, as an MP, or in the judiciary?

NO

YES

Are you the biological father of the baby? and/or are you the mother's husband/partner (see box 1 below)?

AND

Will you have worked for the same employer for 26 weeks by the end of the 25th week of pregnancy, and continue to do so until the birth of the child?

NO →

YES

NO

Sorry – you do NOT qualify for Paternity Leave. You may still qualify for Statutory Paternity Pay, see page 40

Can you say "yes" to all of the following:

will you inform your employer:

- before the end of the 25th week of pregnancy that you intend to take Paternity Leave?
- the week that your baby is expected?
- when you would like your leave to begin?

YES →

Yes, you are entitled to 2 weeks' PATERNITY LEAVE

Box 1: Who qualifies as a "partner"? Someone who lives with the mother of the baby in a long-term relationship but is not a relative. Same-sex partners are included.

count towards continuity of employment. This can only be found on the DTI website at http://www.dti.gov.uk/employment/employment-legislation/employment-guidance/page14391.html

What do I need to tell my employer?

In order to claim either Paternity Leave or SPP you must tell your employer:

- the expected week of the baby's birth
- whether you wish to take 1 week's or 2 weeks' leave
- when you want your leave to start

In addition, in order to claim SPP you must sign a declaration that you:

- are taking leave either to care for your child or to support the mother, or both
- have or expect to have responsibility for the upbringing of the child
- are the father of the child and/or the partner or husband of the mother

You do this using the Form SC3 Statutory Paternity Leave and Pay available on the website accompanying this book.

You are expected to tell your employer when the baby was actually born as soon as is practicable after the birth.

You do not have to provide any medical evidence of the pregnancy or birth.

Employers

If you decide an employee is not entitled to SPP for any reason, you must give them a written statement. You can use Form SPP1 "I cannot pay you Statutory Paternity Pay (SPP)" to do this. It is available from the HM Revenue and Customs Employer's Orderline on 08457 646 646, or can be found on the website accompanying this book.

PATERNITY LEAVE AND PAY

If you can answer YES to all of the questions below, then you are entitled to claim Paternity Leave AND Statutory Paternity Pay	YES	NO
Have you/will you have worked for the same employer for 26 weeks by the end of the 25th week of pregnancy, and continue to do so until the birth of the child?		
Have you/will you inform your employer of the expected week of the birth of the baby?		
Have you/will you inform your employer before the 25th week of pregnancy that you intend to take Paternity Leave?		
Have you informed your employer whether you intend to take one or two weeks' Paternity Leave?		
Have you informed your employer when you want your Paternity Leave to begin?		
Have you/will you tell your employer that you would like to receive SPP at least 28 days before you want it to start?		

Frequently Asked Questions

Do I qualify for Paternity Leave?	To find out if you are entitled to Paternity Leave see page 41
Do I have to provide medical evidence of pregnancy or the birth of the baby?	No, but you must complete Form SC1 to declare your family responsibility and relationship to the mother and child
How much time can I have off?	Up to 2 continuous weeks
Can I have time off to join my partner for antenatal care?	No

When do I have to tell my employer that I want to take Paternity Leave?	By the end of the 25th week of pregnancy
When can I take Paternity Leave?	Not before the birth of the baby. You may choose to start it *either* on the date of the baby's birth *or* on a chosen date after the expected delivery date
How much later after the birth can I take the leave?	Leave must be completed within 56 days of the birth *or* if the baby is premature, within 56 days of the expected birth date.
Can I change the date I want my Paternity Leave to start?	Yes, but you <u>must</u> give 28 days' notice
Can I change the amount of leave I want to take?	No
What happens if the baby is born early?	Give the required information for Paternity Leave and Pay as soon as possible, see page 39
What happens if the baby is born later?	You may not begin Paternity Leave before the baby is born so you must change the start date of your leave
Am I still entitled to paid leave if the baby is stillborn?	Yes, if the baby is stillborn after the 24th week of pregnancy
Am I still entitled to paid leave if the baby dies after birth?	Yes
Will I be paid while on Paternity Leave?	To find out if you are entitled to Statutory Paternity Pay (SPP) see page 40
How much will I be paid?	Either £108.85 a week OR 90% of your average weekly earnings, whichever is lowest

FURTHER INFORMATION

- Both employers and employees can use the DTI interactive guidance site Directgov www.direct.gov.uk/Employment/Employees to work out entitlements to Paternity Leave and Statutory Paternity Pay, or for further general information call the DTI on 020 7215 5000

- For more detailed information see the DTI website at www.dti.gov.uk/employment/workandfamilies/paternity-leave/

- Contact ACAS (Advisory, Conciliation and Arbitration Service) for advice on individual cases and up-to-date advice on employment relation issues; call them on 08457 474747 or visit their website at www.acas.org.uk

- Working Families provide a free legal helpline for low-income families – you can call them on 0800 013 0313 or visit the website at www.workingfamilies.org.uk

- Employers can get more information on SPP from HMRC on their website at www.hmrc.gov.uk/employers

ADOPTION LEAVE AND PAY

This chapter includes information about both Adoption Leave and Pay and Paternity Leave and Pay concerning an adopted child. It outlines the main points that are specific to adopters or partners of adopters claiming Paternity Leave.

3

3 ADOPTION LEAVE AND PAY

Adoption Leave and Pay is available to an eligible employee who adopts a child from the UK or from overseas (although there are some differences in this case, see page 54). Adoption Leave and Pay becomes available when the child is newly placed with you, whether you are an individual adult who is adopting or one member of a couple who are adopting.

If you are part of a couple adopting jointly, you should decide which one of you wishes to take Adoption Leave and Pay. The other member of the couple may be entitled to claim Paternity Leave and Pay. This applies to married couples, and to those living together as partners or civil partners including same-sex couples.

Who qualifies for Adoption and Paternity Leave?

Type of leave	To qualify you must:	Your leave entitlements are:
ADOPTION LEAVE	• be newly matched with a child for adoption by an adoption agency. In circumstances where a child is not "newly matched", for example if you are a step-parent adopting your partner's child, Adoption Leave is not available • have worked for your employer for 26 continuous weeks by or during the week that you receive notification of being matched with a child	• 26 weeks' Ordinary Adoption Leave followed immediately by 26 weeks' Additional Adoption Leave; this is a total of up to 52 weeks' leave • if you have more than one child placed with you as part of the same arrangement, only one period of Adoption Leave is available
PATERNITY LEAVE As the partner, civil partner or spouse in an adopting couple who is not claiming Adoption Leave you may be entitled to Paternity Leave	• have or expect to have responsibility for the child's upbringing • be the adopter's spouse, civil partner or partner • have worked continuously for your employer for 26 weeks by (and including) the week that the adopter receives notification of being matched with a child • continue to work for your employer up to the date the child is placed for adoption • be taking time off to support the adopter and/ or care for the child	• you can take one or two weeks' consecutive Paternity Leave • Leave cannot be taken as odd days or as two separate weeks • only *one* period of Paternity Leave is available, regardless of whether more than one child is placed for adoption as part of the same arrangement

Do I need to provide my employer with evidence?

For Adoption Leave you must supply evidence from the adoption agency that you have been matched with a child for adoption. This would be your matching certificate.

For Paternity Leave your employer may ask you to provide a self-certificate as evidence that you meet the eligibility conditions. A model self-certificate (SC4 Self Certificate Adoption Paternity) can be found on the website accompanying this book.

When can I start my Adoption or Paternity Leave?

ADOPTION LEAVE

You can choose when to start your Adoption Leave. This may be on any day of the week, either:

- from the date of the child's placement (whether this is earlier or later than expected)
  or
- from an agreed date which can be up to 14 days before the expected start of the placement

If you wish to change the start date of your leave, you must tell your employer at least 28 days in advance (unless this is not reasonably practicable).

What happens if the placement breaks down or doesn't work out?

The placement of a child occurs when the child goes to live with the adopter permanently with a view to being formally adopted in the future. So, it may be possible that the arrangement later breaks down. If the child's placement ends during the Adoption Leave period, you can continue Adoption Leave for up to 8 weeks after the end of the placement.

PATERNITY LEAVE

You may start your Paternity Leave on any day of the week, either:

- from the first day of the child's placement (whether this is earlier or later than expected)

- from a chosen date after the start date of the child's placement (whether this is earlier or later than expected)
  or
- from a chosen date which is later than the date on which the child is placed with the adopter

If you wish to change the start date of your leave, you must tell your employer at least 28 days in advance (unless this is not reasonably practicable.)

When and what should I tell my employer if I want to take Adoption or Paternity Leave?

You are required to inform your employer of your intention to take Adoption or Paternity Leave within 7 days of being told by your adoption agency that you have (or your partner has) been matched with a child for adoption, unless this is not reasonably practicable.

ADOPTION LEAVE	PATERNITY LEAVE
You must tell your employer:	
• when the child is expected to be placed with you	• the date on which you were told you have been matched with a child
• when you want the adoption leave to start	• when the child is expected to be placed with you
• the date you were told you had been matched with a child	• whether you wish to take one or two weeks' leave
	• when you want your leave to start

Employers

Employers have 28 days in which to respond to an employee's notification of their Adoption Leave plans. An employer must write to the employee, setting out the date on which they expect the employee to return to work if the full entitlement to Adoption Leave is taken. A model letter for doing this can be found on the website accompanying this book. This does not apply to Paternity Leave.

Can I remain an employee while on Adoption or Paternity Leave?

Throughout Adoption Leave (both Ordinary and Additional) and Paternity Leave your employment contract continues. During Ordinary Adoption Leave and Paternity Leave, you are entitled to receive all your contractual benefits except your wages unless your contract of employment provides otherwise. This includes, for example, your right to staff discounts and compensation in the event of redundancy and notice periods. You are also bound by contractual terms relating to notice of any decision by you to terminate your employment.

Can I change the date I start my leave?

You may change the date on which you wish to start your leave but you must give your employer at least 28 days' notice of your intention to do so, that is to say, 28 days before the date on which you had previously stated as being the first day of leave.

Can I return to work before the end of my Adoption Leave?

If you intend to return to work immediately after the end of your Adoption Leave, you do not have to give your employer advance notice.

If you intend to return to work before the end of your Adoption Leave, you must give your employer at least 28 days' notice of the date of your return.

If you do not wish to use your Additional Adoption Leave, you should give your employer 28 days' notice of your return. This is because you are returning to work before the end of your full Adoption Leave allowance.

Will I get my old job back?

Yes, you are entitled to return to the same job on the same terms and conditions following Adoption Leave unless a redundancy situation has arisen. If a redundancy situation arises while you are on Ordinary Adoption Leave or Paternity Leave, you are also entitled to be offered a suitable alternative vacancy.

Unfair dismissal You are protected from experiencing negative or unfair dismissal for reasons relating to taking, or seeking to take, Adoption Leave or Paternity Leave. Employers and employees can phone ACAS for advice on 08457 474747 or consult their website at www.acas.org.uk

STATUTORY ADOPTION AND PATERNITY PAY

Will I be paid during my Adoption Leave?

Yes, you are normally paid if you take Ordinary Adoption Leave. Additional Adoption Leave is usually unpaid, although you may have contractual rights to be paid during this period. You will need to speak to your employer to find this out.

STATUTORY ADOPTION PAY (SAP)

STATUTORY ADOPTION PAY (SAP)	
Do I qualify?	Your average weekly earnings are £84 or more *and*
	you have worked for your employer for 26 continuous weeks by the time you are notified that you have been matched with a child
How much?	£108.85 a week or 90% of your average weekly earnings, which ever is the least
How long is the paid leave?	SAP is paid for up to 26 weeks (Ordinary Adoption Leave period).
	For adopters who are expecting to be matched with a child for adoption after 1 April 2007, this leave is being extended to 39 weeks

PATERNITY PAY

Statutory Paternity Pay (SPP) is paid to eligible employees, by the employer, for up to 2 consecutive weeks.

STATUTORY PATERNITY PAY (SPP)	
How much?	£108.85 a week or 90% of your average weekly earnings, whichever is the least
How long is the paid leave?	One or two consecutive weeks
Do I qualify?	If your average weekly earnings are £84 or more and you must give your employer at least 28 days' notice that you want to take leave

If you do NOT qualify for SAP or SPP, you should contact your adoption agency because you may be able to receive other financial help. Additional financial support may be available through Income Support, Housing Benefit, Council Tax Benefit, Tax Credits or a Sure Start Maternity Grant. Further information is available from your local Jobcentre Plus office or Social Security office (see section 3 of this book 'Financial Support for Working Families').

Employers

By providing a completed self-certificate, employees can satisfy both the evidence and notice requirements for Paternity Leave and pay. Employers are not expected to carry out any further checks.

The recovery of payments Employers can recover some or all the amount of SAP and SPP they pay out in the same way as they can claim back Statutory Maternity Pay (see page 27).

What if my company has its own scheme for leave and pay when adopting?

If your employer offers their own policy on Adoption Leave or Paternity

Leave, you may choose whichever is better for you. You can take either your employers' or Statutory Adoption Leave but not both.

When and what should I tell my employer if I want to claim SAP or SPP?

For SAP (Statutory Adoption Pay)

You must inform your employer at least 28 days in advance of the date you expect any payments of SAP to start, unless this is not reasonably practicable.

You must show your employer your matching certificate. This includes basic information on matching and expected placement dates. Your adoption agency will provide you with this.

For SPP (Statutory Paternity Pay)

You must provide your employer with a completed self-certificate. A model self-certificate for can be found on the website accompanying this book (Form SC4 Self Certificate Adoptive Paternity).

Further entitlements to time off to care for your adopted child

If you would like to organise further time off with your child/children, then you may qualify for:

- Parental Leave – see page 57
- Flexible working hours – see page 64

OVERSEAS ADOPTIONS

There are some differences concerning Adoption and Paternity Leave and Pay for the adoption of children from overseas. Most terms and conditions are the same as those for Adoption and Paternity Leave and Pay given above. The key differences are:

- **Notification period** Employees must notify their employers of their intention to take adoption leave or paternity leave within 28 days of receiving Official Notification*, *or* completing 26 weeks' continuous employment with the employer, whichever is later

- **When to start Adoption Leave** Adoption Leave cannot start before the child enters Great Britain; the latest that Adoption Leave can start is 28 days after the date of the child's entry
- **When to start Paternity Leave** The earliest Paternity Leave can start (whether 1 or 2 weeks) is the date on which the child enters Great Britain. Paternity Leave must only be taken within 56 days of the date that the child enters Great Britain

*What is Official Notification?

Official Notification means a written notification, issued by or on behalf of the relevant domestic authority. This is usually the Department of Health. This says that it is prepared to issue a certificate to the overseas authority concerned with the adoption of the child, confirming that the adopter is eligible to adopt and has been assessed and approved as being a suitable adoptive parent.

Full guidance can be found in "Parents adopting a child from overseas: Rights to leave and Pay" available on the website accompanying this book.

FURTHER INFORMATION

- Both employers and employees can use the DTI website www.dti.gov.uk/employment/workandfamilies/

- You can also use the DTI's interactive guidance site www.direct.gov.uk/Employment/Employees to work out your entitlements to Paternity and Adoption Leave and Pay. For further general information, call the DTI on 020 7215 5000

- For more detailed information on Adoption Leave and Pay, see form PL518: "Adoptive Parents: Rights to leave and pay when a child is placed for adoption within the UK", available on the website accompanying this book

- For more detailed information on Paternity Leave and Pay, see Form PL517: "Working fathers: Rights to Paternity Leave and Pay"; available on the website accompanying this book

- For more detailed information on Adoption and Paternity Leave and Pay for overseas adoptions, see the DTI booklet: "Adoptive Parents: rights to leave and pay when a child is adopted from overseas", available on the website accompanying this book

- The guidance booklets mentioned in this chapter are available from DTI Publications, call the order line on 0870 1502 500 or it can be ordered on the Internet at www.dti.gov.uk/publications. These are also available on the website accompanying this book

- Employers can get more information on SAP and SPP from HMRC www.hmrc.gov.uk/employers who produce an employer's helpbook E16: "Pay and time off work for adoptive parents", (copies available by calling 08457 64 66 46). They also provide online calculators to help you work out SAP and SPP. For additional help, employers may call the employers' helpline on 08457 14 31 43

PARENTAL LEAVE

Parental Leave allows you to spend time with your child.

This chapter outlines who can take time off work and how much leave you can have.

4

4 PARENTAL LEAVE

KEY FACTS

- Up to 13 weeks' Parental Leave for each child.
- Up to 18 weeks' leave if your child is disabled.
- This leave can be taken up to the child's 5th birthday or up to their 18th birthday if your child is disabled.
- Parental Leave is unpaid.
- At the end of Parental Leave you are guaranteed the right to return to the same job as before, or another one of similar status.

What is it?

Parental Leave is the right to take time off work to look after your child. You can use it to spend more time with your children and strike a better balance between work and family commitments.

For example, you might use Parental Leave to:

- spend more time with your child in the early years
- stay with your child while they are in hospital
- look for new schools
- settle your child into new childcare arrangements
- enable the family to spend more time together, for example, when the child goes to to stay with grandparents

Who can claim it?

Mothers and fathers, whether they are the natural or adoptive parents, can qualify for Parental Leave as long as they are employed full- or part-time.

You must either be named on the child's birth certificate or legally have, or expect to have, parental responsibility. You do not have to be living with the child to qualify for Parental Leave.

For more information about who has parental responsibility, see page 8.

You cannot qualify for Parental Leave if you are:

- self-employed
- a member of the police service or the armed forces
- a crew member engaged in share fishing paid solely by the share of the catch

Is Parental Leave paid?

No. Parental Leave is normally unpaid but your employer can pay you if they want to do so.

How much leave can I take?

Each parent can take up to 13 weeks' Parental Leave for each child. This means that both mothers and fathers, if you have twins or adopt more than one child, can have up to 13 weeks' Parental Leave each, for each child.

Parental Leave cannot be transferred between parents. For example, if you use your 13 weeks' Parental Leave but your partner only uses 5 weeks, you cannot use their remaining 8 weeks. Similarly, if a child stops living with one parent to live with another, the Parental Leave cannot be transferred.

If you have a disabled child, you can take up to 18 weeks' Parental Leave.

One week's Parental Leave must be the same as the length of time you normally work a week. For example, if you work Monday to Friday, a week's Parental Leave for you is 5 days. If you normally work Tuesday and Thursday only, then a week's Parental Leave for you is 2 days.

When can I take it?

Parental Leave can be taken up to your child's 5th birthday or up to the child's 18th birthday if your child is disabled. If you are adoptive parents, you can take Parental Leave up to the 5th anniversary of the placement with you or your child's 18th birthday if that is sooner. If your adopted child is disabled, Parental Leave can be taken up to the child's 18th birthday.

Mothers can take Parental Leave straight after Maternity Leave, as long as you give your employer enough notice and you have previously worked for that employer continuously for a year.

What do I have to do to qualify?

You need to have worked for your employer continuously for a year before you can take Parental Leave. Absence from work because of sickness or pregnancy, a temporary lay-off and holiday breaks do not count as breaks in employment, as long as the employment contract runs throughout.

If you change jobs, you will have to work for 12 months with your new employer before you can take Parental Leave.

Employers

If an employee is using Parental Leave for any other purpose, you can deal with the situation using your normal disciplinary procedures.

What evidence do I need to have to prove I qualify?

Your employer can ask to see evidence that you are a parent or that you have, or expect to have, parental responsibility for a child. Evidence could be the child's birth certificate, adoption papers or the date of placement. Where relevant, your employer can ask to see that your child is entitled to Disability Living Allowance.

Will it affect the perks of my job?

The table below indicates whether or not you are able to continue to receive the benefits from your job while you are on Parental Leave.

Employment benefit	Yes	At the discretion of your employer	Frozen while you are on leave
Annual leave	✔ based on 4 weeks a year		
Company discounts		✔	
Company car		✔	
Company mobile phone		✔	
Health club membership		✔	
Pension			✔* (see note below)

* While you are on Parental Leave, any pension rights you have gained prior to your Parental Leave are frozen and start again once you have returned to work.

Will I still have my job when I return to work?

You are guaranteed the right to return to the same job as before you went on leave as long as the leave is less than 4 weeks. If you are on Parental Leave for longer than 4 weeks, you should still be able to return to the same job unless it is not reasonably practicable. In this case you should be offered a similar job of the same or better status as your old job.

What happens if I don't want to return to work after Parental Leave?

You still have to give your agreed notice period while on Parental Leave. Depending on how long your notice period is, you may have to return to work for a short time to work out your notice period.

What if my employer does not have a Parental Leave scheme in place?

If no specific Parental Leave scheme has been set up by your employer, then the basic government Parental Leave Fallback Scheme will apply (see the box below for details). If your employer does have a scheme, then you can choose which one is more favourable to you.

Basic Parental Leave Fallback Scheme

Key Facts

- You must take your leave in blocks of complete weeks, up to a maximum of 4 weeks a year for each child.

- Parents whose child is entitled to Disability Living Allowance, can take leave in periods shorter than a week.

- You must give at least 21 days' notice to your employer giving the start and finish dates of your leave. This notice does not have to be in writing.

- If your employer thinks your leave will disrupt the business, then they can postpone the leave. However, they are not able to postpone the leave for longer than 6 months after the date you originally wanted to start Parental Leave. This does not apply to the leave you take immediately after the birth of your child or adoption leave.

- If, because your leave has been postponed, the period of Parental Leave falls after the child's 5th birthday, then you are allowed to take the leave after this date.

Claiming Income Support while on Parental Leave

Income Support can be paid to people who are on a low income. There are qualifying conditions (for more information on Income Support, see section 3, chapter 13)

In order to qualify for Income Support during Parental Leave, you must satisfy the following conditions:

- you must be receiving Working Families Tax Credit, Disabled Persons Tax Credit, Housing Benefit or Council Tax Credit before taking Parental Leave

- your Parental Leave is unpaid
- the leave should not be more than 13 weeks in total spread over 4 years, you cannot have more that 4 weeks in one year
- the purpose of the leave is to look after your own child who lives with you
- the leave is taken before the child's 5th birthday or up to 5 years from the placement date for adoption
- Note: the above conditions do not apply to you if you are disabled or a lone parent

Working Families' Tax Credit and Disabled Person's Tax Credits

Tax Credits are fixed for 26 weeks regardless of whether you have Parental Leave while receiving it.

FURTHER INFORMATION

- Both employers and employees can use the DTI website www.dti.gov.uk/employment/balancing-work-family-responsible/. You can also use the DTI's interactive guidance site Directgov www.direct.gov.uk/employment/employees/ to work out entitlements to Parental Leave and pay. For further general information call the DTI on 020 7215 5000.

- Contact ACAS (Advisory, Conciliation and Arbitration Service) for advice on individual cases and up-to-date advice on employment relation issues; call them on 08457 474747 or visit their website at www.acas.org.uk

- Working Families provide a free legal helpline for low-income families. You can call them on 0800 013 0313 or visit the website www.workingfamilies.org.uk

WORKING FLEXIBLY
AND WHAT TO DO
IF YOUR CHILD IS ILL

This chapter outlines a variety of different options for working flexibly, which will help you negotiate your working patterns around your family responsibilities.

This chapter also helps you consider what options are available when you need time off to look after, or organise care for, a sick child.

5

5 WORKING FLEXIBLY

AND WHAT TO DO IF YOUR CHILD IS ILL

KEY FACTS

- Parents with children under 6 years, or 18 years if your child is disabled, have a right to request flexible working hours.
- Employers have a right to "refuse" if there is a clear business reason.

Bear in mind that some options may not be applicable to your job, for example, you are not able to work at home if you are a cleaner or work in a factory.

Requesting to work flexibly

The government has recognised that parents with young children need support to help them maintain their jobs at the same time as caring for their children. As a result, as a parent with a child under 6 years of age, or 18 years if your child is disabled, you have a right to request that your working hours change to suit your needs. However, employers have a right to say "no" if they feel the change in your working pattern will affect their business.

From 6 April 2007, the right to request flexible working is being extended to apply to carers of adults.

The table below will help you think about what flexible working options may be available to you.

FLEXIBLE WORKING OPTIONS

Question	If yes	Flexible working options
Do you work in an office?		Flexi-time Job-sharing Part-time hours Pre-retirement Sabbatical Special leave Term-time working V-time working Work at home
Do your workloads fluctuate with peaks/troughs throughout the year?		Annualised hours Flexi-time Part-time hours Sabbatical Special leave Term-time working V-time working
Do you work in a manual job, for example, as a cleaner, in retail, or at a factory?		Job-sharing Part-time hours Sabbatical Shift-working Special leave V-time working
Do you need flexibility in your working hours?		Annualised hours Compressed working hours Flexi-time Part-time hours Self-rostering V-time working

Do you need some time off work to deal with a personal situation such as a child's long-term illness?		Career break Sabbatical Special leave
Do you want to take some time off work to study?		Annualised hours Career break Flexi-time Job-sharing Part-time hours Sabbatical Shift-working Study leave V-time working

There are many different options to help you organise your working hours to suit the needs of your family. Your company may already offer some ways of working flexibly and there may be an internal application procedure you will need to follow. You need to ask your employer about this.

Annualised hours means working out the number of hours that you would work over a year. You can then work more or less hours at different times of the year to suit your workload and home life. For example, you might work shorter hours during school holidays and longer hours during term time. The pay you receive could depend on the hours worked during each pay period.

A **career break** is a period of unpaid leave from work, usually lasting between 6 months and 5 years. You have an agreement with your employer that you will return to your old job or a similar job in the future. Pay and benefits normally cease during this break and you will no longer be an employee.

Compressed working hours allows employees to work their total number of agreed hours over a shorter period. For example, employees might work their full weekly hours over 4 days, rather than 5, or work 9 days a fortnight instead of 10. Employees would be paid for a full-time job but would not receive overtime payments for the extra hours they would work in any one day.

Flexi-time gives employees choice about their actual working hours, which are usually outside certain agreed core times. This means you can vary your start, finish and break times each day. Individuals are paid for the hours that they work. An example may be that you can arrive any time up to 10am, and leave any time after 4pm as long as over a 4-week period you have worked the required number of hours.

Job-sharing involves 2 employees employed on a part-time basis, but working together to cover the duties of a job normally done by 1 full-time person. Both job-sharers receive pay for the hours they work and divide holiday and other benefits accordingly.

Part-time hours has no legal definition but it is usually defined as working fewer than 30 hours a week. In practice it usually means working less than the normal full-time hours at a particular workplace. It can range from working a few hours a week to just less than full time.

Pre-retirement is an arrangement where you work reduced hours as a way of easing into retirement. For example, 6 months before your date of retirement, you may work a 4-day week and 3 months before the date of retirement work a 3-day week. This ensures that you gradually adjust to the time when you will no longer be working. There is no loss of salary during this period.

Sabbatical leave is a period of time off in addition to annual leave, generally awarded on the basis of length of service. Sometimes people are allowed to use the leave as they wish, for example as a long holiday, for voluntary work or to pursue a particular interest. In other cases sabbaticals are used for training or career development. Although some sabbaticals are paid, others may be partially paid or unpaid.

Self-rostering involves the employer working out the number of staff and type of skills needed each day, then letting employees put forward the times they would like to work. Shift patterns are then compiled accordingly, matching staff preferences to the agreed staffing levels as closely as possible. Self-rostering is often used in hospitals and care services.

Shift-working gives employers the scope to have their business open for longer periods than a more traditional 8-hour working day. Employers can extend the use of their plant or facilities by letting staff work one after another through a 24-hour period. Agreed flexible working arrangements may mean that a shift premium is not needed. Many employers are now realising that longer opening hours and more flexible working shifts can be beneficial to business as well as offering employees more choice in their work pattern.

Special leave can be offered by employers for special circumstances such as emergency leave for childcare related problems, bereavement and study leave. This can include an extended period of leave negotiated with your employer. Special leave is usually unpaid.

Study leave is time off for education that is not necessarily related to the job, although it may be to gain a professional qualification.

Term-time working makes it possible for permanent employees to take unpaid leave during school holiday periods. This enables parents who would find it difficult to work during school holiday times to work only during school term times when it is convenient for them.

Voluntary Reduced Working Hours, sometimes known as 'V-time' working, is an option that makes it possible for permanent employees, in agreement with their employer, to temporarily reduce the number of contractual hours they would normally be expected to work for a specified period.

Working from home has been made easier due to new technology. It doesn't have to be on a full-time basis and it may suit parents to divide their time between working at home and their place of work.

Eligibility

To qualify for the right to request flexible working, you must:

- have a child under 6 years or a disabled child under 18 years and be responsible, or expect to be responsible, for the upbringing of the child
- either be the mother, father, adoptive parent, guardian, foster parent or married to or the partner of the child's mother, father, adopter, guardian or foster parent
- request to work flexibly no later than 2 weeks before the child reaches 6 years old (18 if disabled)
- have worked for your employer continuously for 26 weeks

Note: same-sex partners of a biological parent are able to request to work flexibly if they have responsibility for the upbringing of the child.

If you work for an agency or the armed forces you are not eligible for flexible working.

You may only submit 1 application every 12 months.

Making a request for flexible working

The application

You must put an application in writing to your employer to work flexibly. Your application should include:

- a description of your current working pattern (hours/days/times worked)
- a description of the working pattern you would like to work (hours/days/times worked) and when you would like it to start
- how you feel your new working pattern will impact on your employer and your colleagues and how you think that effect can be dealt with
- a statement that you satisfy the relevant criteria and have not made another application during the last 12 months

You can use Form FW(A) Flexible Working Application Form to do this. This form is on the website accompanying this book.

Putting together a business case for working flexibly

As you can only put in 1 application to work flexibly every 12 months, it is important that you present your application clearly, and with as much detail as possible. You need to:

- contact your human resources department to ask for your employer's policy on flexible working and ask whether any other employees are currently working flexibly or part-time
- gather information on people who are doing similar jobs who are working on a flexible basis – you may want to talk to them to find out how they manage their workload, and how they negotiated an arrangement
- suggest solutions to any potential problems they may raise
- you may want to consider requesting a trial period of flexible working, or for a fixed period – your employer may feel more comfortable if

they know it is only for a short time and you then have this time to demonstrate that you can make it work

Meeting to discuss your request

Your employer must hold a meeting with you to consider your proposal within 28 days of receiving your application.

If you wish, you are allowed to have a colleague attend that meeting with you, as long as they work at the same company.

Your employer must write to you within 14 days of the meeting to let you know their decision.

Employers

You can use Form FW(B) Flexible Working Application Acceptance Form on the website accompanying this book for accepting the proposal to work flexibly, or Form FW(C) Flexible Working Application Rejection Form for rejection. If you feel you need more time to consider an employee's application, you can use Form FW(F) Flexible Working Extension of Time Limit Form to apply for an extension.

Withdrawing your application

You can decide to withdraw your application at any time. You should write to your employer informing them of your wish to withdraw your application. Include the date that your application was submitted. You can use Form FW(G) Flexible Working Notice of Withdrawal Form which is available on the website accompanying this book to do this.

If you decide to withdraw your application, you cannot make another application for 12 months from the date of your original application.

Reasons for refusal

Your employer is allowed to refuse your application to work flexibly if they have a clear business case to do so. Their reasons might include:

- incurring additional costs
- a negative effect on the ability to meet customer demand
- unable to reorganise work amongst existing staff

- unable to recruit additional staff
- a negative impact on quality or work
- a negative impact on performance
- there will not be enough work during the times you wish to work
- there are planned structural changes which may affect your current or proposed working times

What can I do if I am refused?

You can appeal against your employers' decision within 14 days of receiving your answer. You must put in writing why you are appealing against their decision.

You can use Form FW(D) Flexible Working Appeal Form that is on the website accompanying this book.

Employers

You can use Form FW(E) Flexible Working Appeal Reply on the website accompanying this book to reply to an appeal.

FURTHER INFORMATION ON YOUR RIGHT TO REQUEST FLEXIBLE WORKING

The DTI booklet about your right to request flexible working is available on the website accompanying this book called PL520 Guidance on your right to request flexible working.

The organisations listed below can help you further with your rights to flexible working. Their contact details can be found in the Useful Organisations section, page 235:

Advisory, Conciliation and Arbitration Service (ACAS)

Citizens Advice Bureau (CAB)

Equal Opportunities Commission (EOC)

Working Families

WHAT CAN I DO IF MY CHILD IS ILL?

Depending on how much time off work you need, whether it is a couple of days, a week or perhaps longer, you should immediately talk to your employer about the best option for you both.

Formal or informal leave?

Your employer may have formal procedures that you have to follow to apply for time off to care for your children. This may include putting an application together for Special Leave, particularly if you would need a lot of time off.

Depending on the situation, your employer may be able to be flexible, allowing you to have the time off, and make up the hours at another time. This would normally be possible if you need only a few hours off, perhaps to make a hospital visit or to make alternative childcare arrangements.

Your options

Short-term (a couple of hours or a day or two)	Long-term (a week or more)
Emergency Leave	Special Leave
Special Leave	Annual Leave
Annual Leave	Parental Leave
Flexible working hours	Compassionate Leave

Both parents can take time off for childcare, but only if the circumstances demand it. For example, if you have been let down by childcare arrangements, then two parents are not required, but if your child goes into hospital, both parents may want to be there.

EMERGENCY LEAVE – TIME OFF FOR DEPENDANTS

You have a right to take a reasonable period of time off work to deal with an emergency involving a dependant, and you will not be dismissed or penalised by your employer for doing so.

A dependant means your husband, wife, partner, child or someone living with you as part of your family.

What counts as an emergency?

An emergency is when someone who depends on you needs your help for any of the following reasons:

- they are ill
- they are involved in an accident or assaulted
- they need you to arrange long-term care for them
- they need you to deal with an unexpected disruption or breakdown in care, such as a childminder or nurse not turning up
- they are going into labour
- the dependant dies and you need to make funeral arrangements or attend a funeral

Emergency leave is time off to help you deal with unforeseen emergencies. If you know in advance that you are going to need time off, you need to speak with your employer about taking another form of leave, because you may be entitled to a period of Parental Leave (see page 57).

How much time can I have off?

You can have as long as it takes to deal with the immediate emergency. For example, if your child falls ill you can take enough time off to deal with their initial needs, such as taking them to the doctor and arranging for someone to look after them. But you'll need to make other arrangements if you want to stay off work longer to care for them yourself.

Will I be paid?

No. There is no requirement for your employer to pay you and therefore the time off is usually unpaid. However, you need to speak to your employer to find out if they will pay you at your usual rate or at a reduced rate while you are on leave. For more information see the booklets called "Time off for dependants – a guide for employers and employees" or "Parental leave: a guide for employers and employees". Both booklets are available on the DTI website www.dti.gov.uk or on the website accompanying this book.

Can anyone get time off?

This legislation does not apply to the following groups of people:

- the self-employed
- members of the police force
- crew members engaged in share fishing paid solely by the share of the catch

If you require more time off and your child is under 5 years old, you can make a formal request as part of your Parental Leave entitlement (see page 58).

If there is a dispute, then you can take the matter to an Employment Tribunal. The application form is included on the website accompanying this book (ET1 Claim Form).

BREASTFEEDING AT WORK

Employers are required to make reasonable provisions for female employees who wish to breastfeed.

6

6 BREASTFEEDING AT WORK

KEY FACTS

- There should be a degree of flexibility in your working hours and conditions to allow you to continue breastfeeding (unless there are genuine business reasons why you cannot work different hours).
- Your employer should provide rest facilities.
- Your employer must give you protection from health and safety risks.

Am I allowed to continue breastfeeding once I return to work?

All employers have a legal duty to consider how they can support you if you are breastfeeding, unless there are valid business reasons why this is impossible.

Your employer must provide adequate rest, meal and refreshment breaks for women who have given birth in the last six months and for women who are breastfeeding.

You must notify your employer in writing that you intend to breastfeed so that an assessment can be carried out to determine if working conditions pose a risk to you or your baby's health.

If an employer refuses to allow you to breastfeed (either outright or by refusing to change your working conditions to allow you to do so) this may be counted as unlawful sexual discrimination and you should seek further advice from your local Citizens Advice Bureau.

Employers are not required to allow mothers to bring their child into the workplace to breastfeed (rather than expressing milk).

What facilities do I need at work?

Your employer is required to provide suitable facilities for a breastfeeding mother to rest, including somewhere for you to lie down. Health and Safety guidelines recommend that facilities should include access to a private room, provision of a clean fridge to store milk, and time off to express milk or breastfeed if the child is nearby, for example, in a work crèche or you work close to home.

FURTHER INFORMATION ON BREASTFEEDING AT WORK

For further information, the "Health and Safety Executive Guide for New and Expectant Mothers" booklet can be found on the website accompanying this book.

CHILDCARE OPTIONS

section
two

section two

INTRODUCTION TO CHILDCARE SECTION

Choosing and finding the right childcare to suit your family needs can take time. Understanding the benefits and disadvantages of each type of care, and finding a provider near you, can often prove difficult. This section is designed to guide you through the options you have to help you make the right decision for you and your child.

Chapter 7 provides **general guidelines** to consider **when choosing childcare**. This includes some dos and don'ts and questions to think about when searching for the most suitable childcare for your needs.

If you decide that you want to have childcare in your own home then the **childcare in your home** chapter 8 presents the options available. This includes advice on how to find the right person and other considerations you must be aware of, such as the necessity of becoming an employer.

The **out-of-home childcare** chapter 9 gives the variety of options you have to choose from. Depending on the age of your children and the hours you need childcare, this chapter will help you work out what childcare is available to you, and how to find it in your area.

If you have a **child with Special Educational Needs**, you will have additional considerations when choosing childcare. Chapter 10 aims to help you work out your options and consider the support that is available to you and your child.

CHOOSING CHILDCARE: GENERAL GUIDELINES

Choosing childcare or early education is a big decision for any family. There are many different childcare options to choose from, whether based within your home (home-based) or out of your home. This chapter provides some general guidelines that you may want to think about when deciding what childcare will best suit your family needs.

7

7 CHOOSING CHILDCARE: GENERAL GUIDELINES

THE RANGE OF CHILDCARE PROVISION

The different types of home-based and out-of-home childcare covered in this book are:

CHILDCARE IN YOUR HOME	OUT-OF-HOME CHILDCARE
Nanny	Childminder
Au Pair	Nursery Classes and Schools
	Day Nurseries
	Playgroups/Pre-schools
	Parent and Toddler Groups
	Out-of-School Services

For each type of care outlined in the following 2 chapters, you will find the following information:

- the nature of a particular type of childcare (who or what they are)
- the hours of care they provide
- the age of children it is appropriate for
- how much it will cost (approximate guidelines only)
- how you can be assured of the quality of care
- how to find childcare in your area

In addition, there are some suggested questions you may want to ask potential childcare providers so that you can decide whether a particular type of care would suit your needs.

FREE PART-TIME EARLY LEARNING AND CARE FOR ALL 3- AND 4-YEAR-OLDS

Cost is a significant issue for most families when choosing childcare so the Government has introduced free part-time early learning and care for all 3- and 4-year-olds.

What is my child entitled to?	12½ hours a week of free learning and care for 38 weeks a year
When does the entitlement start?	From the first school term (1 September, 1 January, 1 April) following your child's third birthday
Where can I use my free entitlement?	School nursery classes in a state or private nursery school; at a day nursery; at a playgroup or at pre-school; with childminders who are part of an approved Childminder Network
How can I find out more?	Contact your local Children's Information Service (CIS) via ChildcareLink on 0800 096 02 96 or www.childcarelink.gov.uk

GENERAL ADVICE

The table below lists some suggestions for choosing and arranging your childcare:

DOs	DON'Ts
• Do research all the options available to you. Your local Children's Information Service is a good place to start for a list of registered childcarers in your area.	• Don't leave it until the last minute. Give yourself plenty of time to research the options. Popular places will have long waiting lists, and it can take months to find the right carer.
• Do think of some initial requirements, for example, opening hours, costs, location, whether you have to pay a retainer for the place if you are on holiday, and make these your first questions when you phone around.	• Don't rule out combining different types of care. It may be more practical to mix and match, as well as making the most of different types of care for your child's development.
• Do shop around, making appointments to visit several options. Take some prepared questions with you. (The relevant sections in the following chapters will help you with this.)	• Don't feel guilty or awkward about double checks. Go back for second and third looks once you have a shortlist of options.
• Do check every childcarer's references.	
• Do put it all in writing, either in a contract/letter provided by the nursery, or by writing a contract yourself for a nanny/childminder.	• Don't be afraid to make unexpected occasional visits to the childcare setting: arrive early to see what's happening, talk to other parents or carers.
• Do talk to your child everyday to monitor your child's welfare once you have set up childcare. You may ask the carer to keep an activities diary.	• Don't ignore your gut instincts – after all, you are the expert on your child. Think about their personality and age, especially for children under 2 who require a close one-to-one relationship.
• Do book time with the carer a couple of months into the arrangement to discuss your child's progress.	
• Do check if they are registered or not (see pages 85-6). This may affect whether you can get help with funding for the nursery place.	

SURE START

Sure Start is the government programme for delivering the best start in life for every child. This provides checklists for all childcare which suggest aspects for you to consider when you are choosing your provider. The basics are included in this book, but for more detail and to download a copy of Sure Start's booklet "Looking for Childcare?" booklet visit their website at www.surestart.gov.uk/aboutsurestart/parents/lookingforchildcare

REGISTERED OR NON-REGISTERED CHILDCARE?

Whether or not the childcare service needs to be registered depends on the region and age group catered for. If care is provided for more than 2 hours a day, the following out-of-school care services must be registered and inspected:

- in England and Wales: services catering for children aged 8 or under
- in Scotland: services catering for children aged 16 or under
- in Northern Ireland: services catering for children aged 12 or under

What is the difference between registered and unregistered childcare?

Registered childcare is registered and inspected by government inspecting bodies and has to meet National Standards by law.

Note: if you qualify for help with childcare costs through Tax Credits (see chapter 11), it can only be used for registered and approved care.

Does all childcare have to be registered?

No. In **England and Wales** the National Standards apply to childcare for children aged 8 or under, for 2 or more hours that is not based in the child's own home. This includes day nurseries, sessional day care, childminders, out-of-school care, and crèches. Nannies, au pairs and babysitters do not have to be registered. But note that in England and Wales, if a nanny cares for the children of 2 or more families, they do have to be registered.

In **Scotland**, any daycare for children under the age of 16 that is not based in the child's own home has to be registered. But note that if a nanny cares for the children of 3 families or more they do have to be registered.

In **Northern Ireland**, childcare for children under 12 that is not based in the child's own home has to be registered.

Who does the registering?

England, Scotland, Northern Ireland and Wales have their own inspecting bodies who check childcare facilities before they can be registered.

Country	Childcare inspectors
England	Office for Standards in Education (Ofsted)
Wales	The Care Standards Directorate
Scotland	The Scottish Commission for the Regulation of Care
Northern Ireland	The Health and Social Services Trust. Each local trust registers the childcare providers in the area, and the Regulation and Improvement Authority inspects the local trusts to ensure that they are registering properly

Where can I find previous inspection reports?

In **England**, reports on daycare providers in your area are available on the Ofsted website at www.ofsted.gov.uk or you can call them on 08456 404045.

In **Wales**, there is a database with inspection reports of service providers in your local area that you can search. The website is www.csiw.wales.gov.uk/dataviewer/index.asp or you can call them on 08443 848450.

In **Scotland**, reports for inspections carried out after 1 April 2005 will be available online at www.carecommission.com as they are completed. Reports for inspections completed between April 2002 and March 2005 can be obtained from local offices or by using the information request form on the Care Commission website. You can search for a service and inspection report by either entering the service provider's name or by selecting a type of service and the town/region you are interested in. Alternatively, you can call the Care Commission on 0845 6030890.

In **Northern Ireland**, the local Health and Social Services Trusts have the inspection reports so you need to contact each trust individually. You can visit their website at www.dhsspsni.gov.uk/hss/index.asp or call the Department of Health, Social Services and Public Safety on 02890 520500.

APPROVED CHILDCARE

What is approved childcare?

The Childcare Approval Scheme gives recognised national status for individuals providing childcare that does not require registration and is provided in the child's own home, or for children aged over 7 on other domestic premises. If you employ a carer who is approved under the scheme, you may be entitled to get help with costs (see chapter 14).

- An approval certificate is valid for 12 months
- The body which has been appointed to conduct the assessment is Nestor
- The scheme is voluntary and only operates in England

In order to be approved, childcare providers must:

- be aged 18 years or over
- have either a recognised childcare qualification or have attended a valid induction course
- hold a first aid certificate that is less than 3 years old and suitable for the care of babies and young children and covers emergencies, resuscitation, shock, choking and anaphylactic shock
- be able to demonstrate that there is nothing in their past which would suggest that they are unsuitable to care for children (usually via a Criminal Records Bureau check)

For more information on the Childcare Approval Scheme, there is a national helpline available Monday to Friday 9am to 5pm on 0845 767 8111 or visit www.childcareapprovalscheme.co.uk

FURTHER INFORMATION

In the section Useful Organisations there is a comprehensive list of contact details for agencies and organisations that provide information on childcare provision and a wide range of services to support parents and carers in making the right decision.

You can obtain copies of childcare and early education checklists by visiting www.surestart.gov.uk/lookingforchildcare or call 0870 0002288.

The following can provide further information on childcare options and their contact details are available at the back of this book (see pages 235-60):

- Daycare Trust
- Sure Start
- 4Children
- Your local Children's Information Service
- Children in Scotland
- Children in Wales
- Childcarelink

CHILDCARE IN YOUR HOME

This chapter outlines the options you have if you want childcare provided in your own home. Home-based childcare includes nannies and au pairs. Carers may live with you or come to your home every day.

8

8 CHILDCARE IN YOUR HOME

This chapter aims to provide you with the following information about the different types of childcare you can have at your home:

- what the different types of childcare are
- typical hours they provide care
- approximate costs
- how you can ensure quality of care
- how to find a suitable carer

Who is home-based care suitable for?

Home-based childcarers are especially suited to parents who work irregular hours (for example, those who return home late and/or have early starts), to parents whose children have special needs, and/or to those who wish to have their child, or children, cared for in their own home.

Since nannies, au pairs and home-helpers often live in your home, be aware that there are drawbacks such as loss of privacy and extra costs in terms of household bills, food etc. More specific information to help you decide if this type of care is for you is provided in each section below.

HAVING A NANNY

Who is a nanny?

A nanny is someone you employ directly to look after your children in your own home. There are a number of different arrangements possible:

- **a live-in nanny** stays in your home and will need a private bedroom and food in addition to their salary

- **a daily nanny** comes to your home to look after your children
- **nanny-share arrangements** mean that you share a nanny with another family; the nanny may look after your child on certain days and other people's on other days, or may look after both sets of children together

Some nannies (but not all) may also agree to undertake other jobs around the house such as cooking and cleaning.

What age group will a nanny care for?

Nannies can look after children of any age.

What hours can a nanny provide care?

These arrangements may vary depending on whether they live in or are part-time but, generally, nannies work flexible hours to fit in with your needs.

How can I be sure of the care quality?

Nannies do not have to be registered unless they look after the children of 2 or more families in England and Wales, or children of 3 or more families in Scotland.

Most nannies (and some other home-based carers) have a childcare qualification or nursery nurse training, although this is not compulsory.

If you find and employ a nanny yourself, then it is up to you to check their qualifications and references. If you use an agency to find a nanny, then they should do this for you.

How much will it cost?

Nannies can cost between £127 and £400 per week. This varies with their experience, agreed duties, where you live and whether they live with you or come to your home daily. Nannies must be paid at least the National Minimum Wage (see page 183 to find out how much this is). On top of their salary, because you are employing them, you also have to pay their income tax and National Insurance contributions.

Example of extra costs of a nanny

For a nanny earning £28,171 (the average wage in central London), your National Insurance contributions would be £2,979, which makes a total of £31,150 per year.

Using the Childcare Voucher Scheme, it is possible for you to reduce this by up to £2,132 a year through tax relief, see chapter 14.

Other extra costs could include holiday and sick pay, a mobile phone for emergencies and putting them on your car insurance if you want them to drive the family car. You will also need to take out employer's indemnity insurance in case of an accident.

Help with paying your nanny

HMRC Employer Helpline can give advice and calculate tax and NI contributions for you: call 0845 6070143

For a small fee a company called Nanny Tax will deal with paying your nanny's tax and NI, and also issue payslips for you. Call: 0845 226 2203 or visit: www.nannytax.co.uk

If your nanny is approved through the Childcare Approval Scheme (see page 87), some working parents and disabled people may be entitled to help with childcare costs, for example, through Child Tax Credit (see page 140).

Would a nanny suit my needs?

Have a look at the statements below. If you agree with most of them, then a nanny may be a good childcare option for you.

I agree that:

- I need someone to fit around my lifestyle and routine
- I work awkward hours/shifts
- my child has a disability or other special needs
- I want a big say in how my child is cared for and in setting the rules
- transport is a problem for me
- I've got children of different ages to find care for and I'd like them to be together
- I'd like my child to get more one-on-one attention
- my child will be happier in their own home
- I need someone full time as my child isn't at school
- I'd like someone who might also help with housework
- I'm happy to take on the financial and legal responsibilities of employing someone
- I have the correct insurance cover for employing someone
- I have the space and am happy to share my home/privacy with someone

I can put up with these potential disadvantages:

- some nannies are young, have little experience or no qualifications
- it may be expensive especially if the care is for only one child
- nannies may change jobs and may not offer long-term continuity
- there will be extra expenses because the house is occupied all day, such as heating
- the nanny may have visitors to my house while I am not there

How do I find a nanny?

There are a number of ways you can find a nanny:

- call the **National Childbirth Trust** on 0870 444 8707 for local branches with a nanny-share register

- **other parents** – nothing beats a personal recommendation; ask other parents if they know of a good nanny locally

- **advertising** – put an advert in your local paper detailing what you require, or answer an advert put in by a nanny; you could also advertise in national magazines such as *Nursery World* and *The Lady* or at colleges where nannies are trained, or a school notice board is also a good place to advertise for a nanny share.

- **nanny agencies** – there will be a fee involved but the agency should have screened their nannies to make sure they are suitable (ask whether this has been done) and may be able to provide you with someone quickly.
  The Recruitment and Employment Confederation can provide details of reputable nanny agencies in your area, call 020 7462 3260 – always remember that nanny agencies do not have to be registered themselves

- in England, Scotland and Wales, you can find out about registered nannies in your area, from your local **Children's Information Service** www.childcarelink.gov.uk or freephone 08000 960 296);
  in Northern Ireland, call **Employers for Childcare** on 0800 028 3008 or visit their website www.employersforchildcare.org

- if you are looking for another family to share a nanny with, you can register your details with **Sharingcare** who will match your details with other families in your area; visit their website at www.sharingcare.co.uk

What should I ask a prospective nanny?

You should always interview applicants. Here are some suggested questions:

Question	Why ask this?
What qualifications or training do you have?	Not all nannies will have official qualifications
Have you been approved through the Childcare Approval Scheme? (see page 87)	If so, ask to see their letter of approval
Do you have first aid training? (If so, ask to see the certificate)	If so, ask to see their certificate to make sure it is still in date
What kind of experience do you have?	You need to know whether they have looked after children of this age or this number of children before
Why do you enjoy the job?	This will tell you something about their motivation for working with children
Why do you want this particular job?	Find out what appeals to them, is it the age/gender of the child or purely the location of the job
How would you organise my child's day? And how would you help them achieve developmental goals?	This will help you decide if they have the same vision as you
Will you keep a food and day diary?	This may be important if you are trying to establish a routine or watch your child's behaviour and/or food intake
Where would you take my child out?	Establishes whether they they know the local area
How do you feel about early starts/late finishes?	Establishes whether they are flexible to meet your needs
Can you babysit in the evenings?	Establish if they are willing to meet your needs
What's your policy on toilet training, feeding, teaching right from wrong?	Establishes whether it is the same as yours and if they're willing/able to adopt your parenting ideas

Question	Why ask this?
If living in: how will you spend your time off? (You need to be clear on issues like smoking, use of the telephone, having boyfriends/girlfriends/partners to stay.)	It is easier to establish this before they move in, to avoid them moving out again if they or you are not happy
If applicable: would you be happy to carry out extra work such as laundry or housework?	It is best to establish what will be expected of them before they start work

When you have found a nanny you are happy with, it is recommended that you check their references and talk to at least 2 previous employers.

How do I write a contract?

It is important to put everything in writing. Your contract should include the following:

- a job description and hours of work
- salary and agreed method of payment
- length of employment (for example, a minimum 6-month contract) and notice period for you and them to end the contract
- details of sick/holiday pay, expenses paid
- you may wish to add personal childcare practice stipulations, such as how much TV watching, how many sugary treats or drinks and so on

The Professional Association of Nursery Nurses (PANN) issues a Nanny Pack, which includes a sample contract and other useful information for you as an employer. This is available for £5 and can be ordered from them by calling 01332 372337 or from their website www.pat.org.uk

FURTHER INFORMATION

ParentsCentre can give you advice and guidance; visit their website at www.parentscentre.gov.uk/familymatters/childcare/findananny

AU PAIRS

Who are they?

An au pair is an overseas visitor aged between 17 and 27 who comes to the UK on a cultural exchange programme to learn another language and help out in a family home. An au pair will live in your house as part of your family and is entitled to a private bedroom and meals.

Nationals of the EU can enter the UK without any formal restrictions, but due to the fact that some au pairs are from overseas, there are **legal requirements** that apply:

- au pairs from outside the EU[1] must have a special visa that is usually valid for a year and will restrict what they can do
- au pairs from outside the EU should not stay in the UK for more than two years

What hours can they work?

You can expect an au pair normally to work a maximum of 25 to 30 hours per week, depending on the rules in their country of origin, and they must have time off to attend language classes.

How much will it cost?

You should pay an au pair a reasonable weekly allowance. Minimum wage laws do not apply to au pairs but the Home Office sets a minimum, currently this is £55 a week.

Would an au pair suit my needs?

In addition to the pros and cons of having someone else live with you in your house, you should consider the following advantages and disadvantages:

1   Countries in the EU are Austria, Belgium, Cyprus, Czech Republic, Denmark, Estonia, Finland, France, Germany, Greece, Hungary, Ireland, Italy, Latvia, Lithuania, Luxembourg, Malta, Netherlands, Poland, Portugal, Slovakia, Slovenia, Spain, Sweden, United Kingdom.

ADVANTAGES	DISADVANTAGES
Costs are low	They are usually not trained in childcare
They are an affordable after-school care option	Au pairs can only work limited hours, about 5 hours a day or 25 hours a week
Your child can be looked after at home	Au pairs usually stay only 6-12 months
If you have more than one child, they can be looked after together, even if they are of different ages	Au pairs should be treated as a family member – you'll almost certainly need to provide some emotional support for a young au pair
They can often babysit at short notice	There may not be a chance for an interview with an au pair
They may help with some housework	You may have to arrange English lessons for them
Au pairs can teach your child a new language and about another culture	Depending on their knowledge of English, there might be language or communication difficulties
A good au pair can become a close friend	It's your responsibility to make sure they know the basics of childcare, first aid techniques and have emergency back-up

What should I ask a prospective au pair?

There may not be an opportunity to interview an au pair but if there is, some of the questions suggested for interviewing a prospective nanny may be useful (see page 95). You may also want to put agreements with your au pair in writing, to include hours of work, job description, length of employment, house rules etc.

What age group can au pairs care for?

All ages for short periods but as they are usually quite young, they shouldn't be left in sole charge of pre-school children for long periods.

How can I be sure of the quality of childcare I will get?

Au pairs, home-helpers and babysitters are not registered with government regulatory bodies, are not usually trained and will almost certainly have no childcare qualifications. You are therefore responsible for ensuring the quality of childcare they provide. It's also a good idea to give any of these carers the opportunity to be able to call on a responsible adult if necessary. You should make sure you check references and speak to any previous employers.

How do I find an au pair?

There are several ways to do this:

- **agencies** Look in your local phone book for an au pair agency. Choose one that's a member of either the International Au Pair Association (IAPA) or the Recruitment and Employment Confederation (REC), as these agencies vet their applicants; you can also visit the IAPA website www.iapa.org or email them at mailbox@iapa.org

  The REC has a Childcare Sector Group, which is made up of REC member agencies who deal almost exclusively in the placement of nannies and au pairs, and who adhere to the Nanny Codes of Practice and/or the Au pair Codes of Practice; for further information about issues concerning hiring an au pair, you can visit the website at www.rec.uk.com or call them on 020 7462 3260

- **magazines and newspapers** Many nannies, au pairs or agencies advertise in newspapers, or you can place your own advert; always check references and speak to previous employers

- **other parents** Nothing beats a personal recommendation; ask other parents if they know of a good local au pair

CHILDCARE OUT OF THE HOME

If you do not want to, or are unable to employ childcare in your own home, here are the different options available when choosing the right childcare to suit your needs out of your home.

9

9 CHILDCARE OUT OF THE HOME

There are many different types of childcare available outside the home, so when deciding whether out-of-home care would be your best option, you need to consider what type of childcare would best suit you and your child. This chapter aims to help you choose, and covers the following types of childcare:

- parent and toddler groups
- playgroups/pre-schools
- nursery classes and schools
- day nurseries
- childminders
- out-of-school childcare services

The following tables aim to help you establish which type of home care is most suitable for you and your child. Use the first table to work out what childcare options are available, based on your child's age.

OUT OF HOME CHILDCARE OPTIONS BY AGE OF CHILD

Age of your child	Childminder	Nursery school / class	Day nursery	Playgroup	Parent & Toddler group	Out of school care
Pre-school	✔	✔	✔		✔	
3–4 years	✔	✔	✔	✔		✔
5–11 years	✔					✔
11–14 years	✔					✔

Now consider the list of statements in the next table to work out what are the most important issues for you and your child.

WHAT TYPE OF OUT OF HOME CHILDCARE ARE YOU LOOKING FOR?

	Childminder	Nursery school / class	Day nursery	Playgroup (Pre-school)	Parent & Toddler group	Out of school care
I need somewhere that has flexible start/finish times	✔					
I want my child to be taught my qualified teachers		✔	✔			
I want to get involved with my child's childcare				✔	✔	
I only need a few sessions a week	✔	✔	✔	✔	✔	✔
I want my child to follow a set learning curriculum		✔	✔			
I need care that is available all year round (eg not just term time)	✔		✔	✔	✔	
I want my child to be with a small group	✔					
I want my child to be with a registered provider	✔	✔	✔	✔		✔ depends on the service offered
My child is aged 3–4 years and I want to use my free place	✔ only if childminder is part of an Approved Childminder Network	✔	✔	✔		
I need childcare all day while I am at work	✔					✔

Questions to think about

Early education and pre-school services can differ, as can individual childminders, nurseries, nursery classes and before/after school clubs. It is a good idea to leave enough time to visit several childcare options in your local area. You may want to take your child with you, to see how staff interact with him/her. Also, visiting when children are there will give you the best idea of what's on offer, allowing you to see for yourself if the children are happy, engaged in what they are doing and calm.

Be prepared to ask lots of questions, which childcare providers should be happy to answer. Here are some suggestions:

Questions to ask your childcare provider	Things to think about
How long have staff been working in the setting?	Stability and continuity of relationships are important to a child's development
What training and qualifications do the staff have?	The National Standards outline minimum qualifications for staff in day care facilities. For more information on required standards in England and Wales visit www.surestart.gov.uk/improvingquality
	For information on care in Scotland go to the Scottish Executive website at www.scotland.gov.uk/publications/2002/04
	In Northern Ireland contact the Social Care Council on 02890 417600 or visit their website on www.niscc.info
Can I look round the building to see the rooms and outside play space? If there is no outside play space, how will you make sure my child gets the chance to play outside?	Settings need to be safe, welcoming and stimulating. Look for a variety of toys and materials, stored so that children can get at them easily; clean toilets with hand dryers or disposable paper towels; and enough space so children can move around without falling over each other; check if there is outside space
Where can my child rest?	Rest areas should be quiet, dimly lit and have soft furnishings

Questions to ask your childcare provider	Things to think about
What kind of food and drink will you give? Do I have to provide any food for my child?	Children should have access to fresh fruit and vegetables and water when they need it
What will my child do all day? Is there a clear routine for children?	Daily activities should be interesting and varied, including quiet and active, with some opportunities for children to choose
How many children do you look after and how much individual attention will my child receive?	See pages 111, 113 and 118 to find out more about the required number of adults for different aged children in different settings
Will my child be with a regular group of children?	Friendships are important to children and being part of a regular group can help. However, flexibility of timetabling and opportunities to mix with older and younger children can also be beneficial
How will you make sure I know how my child is getting on?	You should expect regular meetings with your child's carer and/or the person responsible for collecting and co-ordinating information on their development
How do you deal with difficult and challenging behaviour?	Providers should have a written policy for this. Look out for strategies focussing on understanding rather than reprimanding a child, as these are indicators of effective behaviour policies
Do you have a routine for settling my child in with you?	Check whether they want you to stay with your child for the first few sessions
Are they willing to fit in with your ideas on discipline, toilet teaching, television watching, sweets and other issues?	This is particularly applicable for childminders

Questions to ask your childcare provider	Things to think about
What happens in the case of an emergency or accident? What safety procedures do they have in place?	Find out how many emergency contact numbers they want and what happens if they are unable to get hold of you at any time
What happens if I am late to pick up my child?	Establish whether someone will remain with your child and find out if you will be charged for late pick-ups
What happens if your child is sick? *What happens if one of the carers is sick?*	Ask whether your child is able to attend the childcare facility and if they have back-up staff during illness
Will you have to pay for your child's place when they do not attend?	Establish whether when your child is sick or when you are away on holiday, you need to pay a retainer fee to keep the place

Always take up references. If you do not already have a recommendation, you could also ask for names of other parents to talk to about a particular service. Most importantly, trust your own feelings about the childcare service – after all, you are the expert on your child.

Contracts

Once you have chosen your childcare provider, you will be required to sign a contract/registration form. This should include agreements on:

- if, and how much, you need to pay as a fee or deposit to secure your child's place
- the amount you will pay for the childcare, how often you pay (daily/weekly/monthly) and what the fees cover (for example nappies, food, days out)
- the hours/days your child will attend
- what you pay if your child or the carer is sick
- any late-pick up fees

PARENT AND TODDLER GROUPS

What are they?

Parent/carer and toddler groups provide regular drop-in sessions for children and their parents or carers, where there is a happy, safe and stimulating environment for children to meet, socialise and play.

These groups are often run by the members themselves on a voluntary basis. They are sometimes held on the same premises as pre-schools (although at different times), or at other premises that may be used for different purposes such as in a community hall.

What age and how many children do they care for?

These groups are mainly for pre-school age children, usually under 2½ years. However, since parents/carers stay with the child they can be for any age child. Group size will often vary from week to week.

Are these groups registered?

As parents/carers stay with their children, these groups do not have to be registered.

How much will it cost?

Costs are low and very reasonable, since they are usually voluntary-based groups.

How can I find a parent/carer and toddler group?

Your local Children's Information Service (CIS) may be able to provide you with details of local groups. You can obtain CIS contact details via ChildcareLink: call 08000 960296 or visit www.childcarelink.gov.uk

You can also try your library, local authority, local newspaper or notice boards or at your GP surgery.

Would a parent/carer and toddler group suit my needs?

If you want to work, parent/carer and toddler groups do not provide the type of care that will allow you to leave your child to do other things because you have to stay with your child. However, the groups are often as important to the parents as the children, providing an informal atmosphere and an excellent opportunity to socialise with other parents and carers of similar age children.

PLAYGROUPS/PRE-SCHOOLS

What are they?

A playgroup/pre-school* is a group organised by the community or voluntary groups on a not-for-profit basis. They provide play and education sessions and start children on the Foundation Stage of the National Curriculum.

Playgroups offer the opportunity for you to become involved yourself, either as a helper or as a member of the management committee, or by taking a course or running an activity for the children.

*The term "pre-school" is also used to cover nursery care and to avoid confusion the term playgroup will be used from now on.

What hours do they provide care?

Playgroups are usually only open during school term time. Each session usually lasts about 3 hours. They may be available every day or for only a few days per week. However, an increasing number are beginning to offer extended or full day care.

What age and how many children do they care for?

Children are usually aged between 3 and 5 years, although some playgroups take children from 2 years old.

The average playgroup size is between 10 and 20 children, although some may cater for up to 30.

Are playgroups registered?

Playgroups are registered by government regulatory bodies (for example, Ofsted) and are inspected regularly to check that the quality of care and free part-time early education (if provided) are satisfactory. Half of the staff must be trained and some may be qualified teachers. In practice, most staff will be trained or in the process of training. The table below shows the number of children that can be supervised by each adult, in practice, although the ratio of adults to children is often much higher because many parents help out too.

The required minimum number of adults to children at a playgroup

Age of child	Number of adults	Number of children
3–5 years	1	8
2 years	1	4
under 2 years	1	3

How much will it cost?

Entitlement to free part-time early learning and care for all 3- and 4-year-olds includes the option of a place at a playgroup. For more information on free part-time early learning and care places for 3- and 4-year-olds, see page 83.

Costs are kept to a minimum but on average you can expect to pay £3-£6 for a 3 hour session, although this will vary according to location. Your local **Children's Information Service** (CIS) will be able to give you information on prices in your area.

Would a playgroup suit my needs?

In addition to the benefits that are common to other types of out-of-home care, for example, mixing with other children, developing skills and confidence and qualified carers, there are some specific features of a playgroup setting to consider. Look at the statements in the box below to see if a playgroup would be the right option for you and your child.

If you agree with these statements, a playgroup may be the right choice for you:

- I'd like to get to know the local community better and get to know other parents
- I've got spare time and I'd like to get involved with the playgroup
- I don't want to leave my child longer than I need to
- I want my child to have both play and learning opportunities with other children
- I do not mind that the premises, such as a church hall, may be used for other purposes
- I do not mind that sessions last only 3 hours or that there is no care during school holidays (around 13 weeks)
- I want the playgroup to supplement my other childcare arrangements, for example, my childminder can take my child to playgroup

How do I find a playgroup?

Playgroups are very popular, so start looking for one as soon as possible and put your child's name down early.

If you live in England, Scotland or Wales you can get more information about local playgroups in your area from your local **Children's Information Service** (CIS). You can find out CIS contact details by calling ChildcareLink on 08000 96 02 96 or by visiting the ChildcareLink website www.childcarelink.gov.uk

The following organisations can also provide information on playgroups in each region of the UK:

The Pre-school Learning Alliance
Tel: 020 7833 0991
Website: www.pre-school.org.uk

Wales Pre-school Playgroups Association
Tel: 01686 624573
Website: www.walesppa.org

Scottish Pre-school Play Association
Tel: 0141 221 4148
Website: www.sppa.org.uk

Northern Ireland Pre-school Playgroups Association
Tel: 028 9066 2825
Website: www.nippa.org

You can also ask your Local Authority, your health visitor or doctor, or talk to other parents – nothing beats a personal recommendation.

How do I choose the right playgroup for me and my child?

In addition to the general questions outlined in previous sections, here are some specific questions to bear in mind when choosing a playgroup:

- how much emphasis is placed on parental involvement and how can I be involved?
- can I stay during a session to be sure this type of care is right for my child?
- is the building well-kept, safe and appropriate (especially if it is used for other purposes, for example, a community hall or a church)?
- is there a space for sitting-down activities, an area for free play and an area for more physical activities?
- are the leader and other staff members suitably qualified?
- is there plenty of equipment of a high standard?

NURSERY CLASSES AND SCHOOLS

What are they?

A **nursery school** is separate and independent of schools for older children, but it may have links with a particular school. It has its own headteacher and staff (who will be trained teachers, nursery nurses and classroom assistants).

At the nursery a child will begin the first stage of the National Curriculum, called the Foundation Stage.

There are different types of nursery schools, including:

- **State nursery schools** are funded by the Local Education Authority and usually places are free
- **Community preschools** are independently run on a not-for-profit basis (often by parents). They charge fees, although your child may be entitled to a free part-time place (see page 83)
- **Private nursery schools** are independently run and charge fees, although your child may be entitled to a free part-time place (see page 83).

A **nursery class** is a pre-school class attached to a school for older children. Its head teacher is the head of the entire school. It is staffed by trained teachers, nursery nurses and classroom assistants, who are also part of the main school. It will almost certainly offer a government-approved Early Years teaching curriculum.

There are different types of nursery classes, including:

- **State nursery classes** are attached to a particular state infant or primary school and run by the Local Education Authority; these classes are free
- **Private nursery classes** are attached to a particular private school and charge fees, although your child may be entitled to a free part-time place

What hours do they provide care?

Nursery schools and classes are usually open during school hours (9am to 3.30pm) in term time. Children can attend all day or just part of the day, either a morning or afternoon session of about 2½ hours. Most children are offered part-time places.

What age and how many children can they care for?

Nursery schools and classes cater for pre-school children up to 5 years old. Most take children from 3 years, but some accept younger children.

The size of the school or class will vary but the number of staff will reflect the number of children who attend. For every 26 children (aged 3 to 5 years) there must be at least 2 adults. One of those adults will be a qualified teacher and the other will be a trained nursery nurse or classroom assistant.

How can I be sure of the quality of care?

All nursery classes or schools which receive funding from a Local Authority or Local Education Authority must be inspected to ensure the Early Years education. This would include most nursery schools/classes.

For further information on relevant inspecting bodies, inspections and registered care, see pages 85-6.

How much will a nursery place cost?

You may be entitled to a free place. All 3- and 4-year-olds are entitled to a free part-time early learning and care place. This includes the option of a place in a nursery class or school, either state or privately run, see page 83 for more information.

For any pre-school age child, care is free if the nursery class or school is part of the state education system. If you're choosing a community pre-school, expect to pay around £3.50 per session.

If you're choosing a private nursery school, expect to pay from around £800–£1,200 per term.

DAY NURSERIES

What are they?

A **day nursery** can look after your child all day, either full-time or part-time, and provides care and education. In a day nursery children should experience learning and development suitable for their age.

There are different types of nurseries, including:

- **private nurseries** are independent businesses providing full daytime care and charge fees
- **community nurseries** provide full daytime care and are run on a not-for-profit basis for local families; their fees are generally lower than private nurseries and they may operate a staggered pricing plan where you are able to pay cheaper fees if you have a low income
- **workplace nurseries** are provided by some employers for staff at the place of work

- **Local Authority nurseries** mainly cater for families on a low income (sometimes providing free places) and usually operate between 9am and 3pm

What hours do they provide care?

Day nurseries are open for longer than nursery schools or classes. They are usually open 8am to 6pm every working day, usually Monday to Friday except Bank Holidays.

What age children and how many children do they care for?

Most day nurseries take pre-school children aged 0–5 years but some may take children up to the age of 8 years. Many also offer out-of-school care for 5- to 11-year-olds. Some may accept babies as young as 6 weeks, but others will not take children below a certain age. It is best to ask the nursery about their policy.

The numbers of children in each nursery vary greatly, but it is usually between 25 and 40. Children are often grouped according to age.

The maximum number of children there will be to each adult in a day nursery

Age of child	Number of adults	Number of children
under 2 years	1	3
2 years	1	4
3–7 years	1	8

How can I be sure of the quality of care provided?

At least half the staff must be qualified in an early years discipline, and some must be qualified teachers. All the staff are required to receive basic training in health and safety. It is a legal requirement that all nurseries be registered with government regulatory bodies and be inspected regularly, see pages 85-6 for further information.

How much will a day nursery cost?

If your child is 3- or 4-year-old, they are entitled to a free part-time place in early learning and care; and this can be at a day nursery if you so choose.

If you don't have a free place, the cost will depend on the type of nursery, possibly on your circumstances, and whether or not costs are subsidised by your Local Authority or employer. Private nurseries are usually the most expensive, in contrast to Local Authority nurseries that are often free (or only charge for meals).

Costs also vary according to where you live. On average, the weekly cost of a full-time place is between £100 and £170, but may range between £75 and £250. However, you may be entitled to a free place if your child is a 3- or 4-year-old.

CHOOSING NURSERY CARE: DAY NURSERIES, NURSERY SCHOOLS AND CLASSES

Would some form of nursery care be the right choice for my child?

Yes – a nursery may be suitable if:

- I want my child to be somewhere that is registered and regularly inspected

- I want my child to be taught by qualified teachers

- my child is ready for an appropriate and structured learning programme

- I want my child to be among children of the same age, with the opportunity to make lots of friends

- I need there always to be someone to look after my child, even if one carer may be away

- my child is 3- or 4-year-old and I want to take up a free Early Years childcare place

The nature and environment of care offered by nursery schools/classes and day nurseries have much in common. The statements below may help you decide if nursery care would suit you and your child.

No – a nursery may be unsuitable if I am unhappy that:

- the staff will not be able to care for my child if he/she becomes ill
- there may be a long waiting list for a place
- I may have to live within the catchment area
- there may be fees to pay
- I will have to pick up and drop off my child, which may require transport
- ratios of children to carers are higher than in other settings
- not all children settle well into a busy environment

The table below will help you decide which of the two types of nursery care will be best for you

Nursery Schools/Classes	Day Nurseries
After attending a nursery class, your child may be able to go on to a linked school when reaching the right age	Care for under 2-year-olds can be difficult to find, and it may not be possible for siblings to be looked after together
Nursery care in a state nursery school is free, regardless of your income	Fees may be high, and financial support may be dependant on your circumstances
You may have to find (and pay for) additional cover during holidays and outside school hours	It is usually open all year, and open longer hours than schools/classes, which may fit in with your work or study hours

How do I find a nursery school/class or day nursery?

Some nursery schools/classes and day nurseries have long waiting lists, so you should start looking early.

- if you live in England, Scotland or Wales you can get more information about local nurseries in your area from your local **Children's Information Service** (CIS); you can find out your local CIS contact details by calling ChildcareLink on 08000 96 02 96 or looking on their website www.childcarelink.gov.uk
  If you live in Northern Ireland, call **Employers for Childcare** on 0800 028 3008 or visit www.employersforchildcare.org
- you could also ask your **health visitor or doctor**, your employer (find out if your firm has a workplace nursery), or talk to other parents for a personal recommendation

Nursery schools and classes:

- the **Independent Schools Council** information service (ISCis) can provide a list of independent schools in your area. You can call them on 020 7798 1500 or visit their website at www.isc.co.uk
- your **Local Authority** (LA) can also provide you with information on registered nursery schools and classes.

Day nurseries:

- the **National Day Nurseries Association** can also help you locate day nurseries in your area; contact them by calling 0870 774 4244 or visit their website at www.ndna.org.uk
- you can also look in your **local telephone directory** for a list of local day nurseries; or if you don't have a directory, your local library will have all the phone directories for the area

How do I choose the right nursery school/class?

Nursery schools/classes should let you visit to see what they are like. Try to go when the session is in full swing, and go back for a second viewing. You may want to take your child with you to see how they get on with staff and other children.

Below are some questions you may want to think about when making your decision:

Staff

- are there enough adults/carers for the number of children? (see page 113 for government guidelines)
- do they operate a key carer system (this is where each child is assigned to a particular individual staff member to enhance continuity of care)?
- how long have the staff worked there? (a high turnover of staff could be disruptive)
- do the staff seem happy, relaxed and confident?
- are they approachable and welcoming to my child?
- what are their qualifications and experience?

Environment and equipment

- what kind of food is provided? Can they accommodate special diets?
- is there a safe and clean play area?
- is the equipment clean, safe, good quality and appropriate for my child?
- is there a range of activities to suit my child's age group?
- is the interior bright, warm and welcoming?
- is there an outdoor space?
- do children look happy and well occupied and are they well supervised by staff?

Registration and inspection

- are the certificates of registration and insurance displayed?
- can I look at inspection reports such as recent Ofsted reports?
- does the nursery belong to any professional organisations such as National Day Nurseries Association?

You and your child

- will they keep a record of what my child has done?
- how many children are there of the same age?
- what happens if I am late to collect my child?
- can they pick-up/drop-off from my other childcare arrangements?
- what is the daily routine?
- how can I get involved?
- how will I find out how well my child is settling in?

CHILDMINDERS

Who are they?

Childminders are professional carers who provide care and education based in their own home for children to whom they are not related.

Childminders negotiate a contract with parents and charge a fee for their service. Childminders are not personally "employed" by parents, but instead are self-employed, and take care of their own tax and National Insurance.

What hours do they provide care?

Since childminders are self-employed, they decide their own working hours. Most will provide childcare between the hours of 8am and 6pm. Some will work early mornings, evenings and weekends. Many are happy to provide part-time places.

What age and how many children can they care for?

According to government regulations, a childminder is allowed to look after up to 6 children under the age of 8, including their own (under 12 in Scotland and Northern Ireland). However, of these no more than 3 of those should be under the age of 5, and of those 3, no more than 1 should be under the age of 1 (exceptions are made for siblings).

The maximum number of children each childminder is able to look after

Number of children	Age of child
1	up to 12 months
2	under 5 years
3	
4	under 8 years
5	
6	

How can I be sure of the quality of care?

By law, childminders must be registered and regularly inspected by the Office for Standards in Education (Ofsted). The registering process involves the checking of references, a health check, a police check on the childminder and every adult in their household, and an inspection of the childminder's house to ensure it is a safe and suitable environment for children.

Some childminders may have childcare qualifications but not all childminders will have these. All childminders in England and Wales (although not yet in Scotland and Northern Ireland) are required to complete a basic registration course, which includes first-aid training.

How much will it cost?

Entitlements to free part-time early learning and care for all 3- and 4-year-olds include the option of a place with a registered childminder who is part of an Approved Childminder Network, see page 85 for an explanation of what registered childcare means.

Childminders have the right to set their charges/fees themselves. Fees will vary from area to area. Many offer a discount for the second child from the same family.

How much you can expect to pay

£ per hour		
	Average	Maximum
England & Wales	£2.4	£6
Scotland	£2.45	£4
Northern Ireland	£1.85[1]	£3.5

1   This is a recommended minimum

Contracts with childminders

You'll need to agree a contract with your childminder to cover hours, fees, food and transport, holidays and sickness arrangements, overtime or late pick-up. The Northern Ireland Childminding Association (NICMA) publishes a guide to help childminders and parents set fees and draw up contracts. This is available for £2 on their website at www.nicma.org or call them on 02891 811015.

Would a childminder suit my needs?

To help you decide if a childminder is the right childcare for you, consider the statements below:

ADVANTAGES	DISADVANTAGES
Childminders are registered, inspected and may have childcare qualifications	Childminders will probably want to organise their daily routine to suit their own lifestyle rather than yours
Childminders are often more flexible than nurseries	A childminder may not be flexible about hours
The childminder may be able to pick up/drop off to other care arrangements	A childminder may not be prepared to pick up/drop off your child at other care arrangements
Your child will be able to play with and interact with other children	There is likely to be a range of ages – you need to decide if this is appropriate for your child
Your child is cared for in a small group, with attention to individual needs	A childminder probably won't be able to care for your child when he/she is ill
Siblings of different ages may be looked after together	Your child has to be taken there and collected
Usually it's cheaper than a nursery	You may be unable to claim free early learning and care entitlement for your 3- or 4-year-old if the childminder is not part of an approved childminder network
The childminder may form a stable and on-going relationship with your child, from baby- to school-age care	

How do I find a childminder?

It may take a while to find the right childminder, one that you are happy with and has space for your child, so it is a good idea to start looking early:

- your local **Children's Information Service** (CIS) will have details of registered childminders in your area; to get their contact details you can visit their website www.childcarelink.gov.uk or call free on 0800 0960296 (this doesn't include Northern Ireland)

- alternatively, you can call the **National Childminding Association** for more information on childminder networks: 0800 169 4486 or visit www.ncma.org.uk

- in **Northern Ireland** you can also contact the Northern Ireland Childminding Association, who have a Childminding Information and Vacancy Service. Their website is www.nicma.org or call them on 028 9181 1015

- in **Scotland** the Scottish Childminding Association gives advice on all aspects of childminding; you can visit their website www.childminding.org or email information@childminding.org or call 01786 449063 for more information; for a list of registered childminders in your local area you should contact your local Care Commission

- **word of mouth** – colleagues, friends or family may be able to recommend a childminder or they might know about one who will have a place available shortly but who has not yet advertised this through the Children's Information Service (CIS)

How do I choose the right childminder for me and my child?

To help you choose the right childminder for your child, the **National Childminding Association** (NCMA) has produced a guide, which is available free on their website. This includes information on: starting early, shortlisting, contacting the childminder, visiting the childminder, questions to ask the childminder, fees, contracts and settling in your child. This guide is available on their website www.ncma.org.uk/download/choosecm.pdf or call them on 0845 8800044. A copy can also be found at the website accompanying this book.

Some questions to ask a prospective childminder:

- working hours: when is the childminder available to work, how flexible are these hours?
- how much do they charge?
- what do they do when children are naughty?
- what activities are provided, including any trips out of the house?
- school and nursery runs – can they pick up and/or drop off children?
- food – what kind of drinks and snacks are available?
- what are the transport arrangements?
- what training or relevant qualifications do they have?
- can I look at any registration, insurance certificates, Ofsted inspection reports, references from other parents?

OUT-OF-SCHOOL CARE SERVICES OR KIDS' CLUBS

What are they?

Out-of-school care services or kids' clubs offer play facilities and supervision of school age children, provided by a team of staff, usually called 'play workers'. These can include:

- **breakfast clubs/before school clubs** that are open in the morning before school so children can enjoy breakfast there
- **after school clubs** that are open in the afternoons between end of the school day until early evening
- **holiday play schemes** that are open during school holidays between about 8.30am and 6pm and may be run by voluntary organisations,

Local Authorities or charities in local parks, community centres, leisure centres or schools

During what hours do they provide care?

Before and/or after school and/or all day during school holidays. Usually their opening hours are roughly the same as working hours between 8am and 6pm.

What ages and how many children do they care for?

The number of children varies greatly and depends on where the service is provided, with most offering between 10 and 40 places.

Out-of-school services may offer care for children from the age of 3 years and upwards (to fit around nursery/pre-school care), but most children are aged 5–11 years old. Some services provide places geared for older children aged 10–14 years, and sometimes for children aged 15–16 years with special needs.

How can I be sure of the quality of care provided?

At least half of the staff must hold a level 2 qualification appropriate for the care and development of children. There are also rules on the number of staff that have to be available for the number of children, see page 113. Registered out-of-school services must have regular checks to ensure the premises are safe and that a suitable service is being provided.

How much will it cost?

The cost will vary according to where you live, and the type of out-of-school care services. As a rough guide, average costs are:

- After school or kids' club place – £3-£10 per day
- Breakfast club place – around £1 per day
- Holiday play scheme – around £15 per day, or £75 per week

Some clubs make fundraising efforts to keep costs down, and some may offer reductions for siblings or for children of lone parents.

Would an out-of-school service suit my needs?

The table below outlines some of the advantages and disadvantages of choosing out-of-school care services for your child.

Advantages	Disadvantages
It is geared to the needs of children with working parents, bridging the awkward gap between school and work hours	Opening hours can be inflexible
Enables children to learn, relax and have fun after school	Your child might want to get away from school at the end of the day
Your child can mix with older and younger children, and may have friends who also attend	There may be maximum/minimum age limits and siblings may not be included
Many out-of-school care services will offer part-time places	Out-of-school care services can be very busy, which may not suit your child and this may be overwhelming for a younger or shyer child
Staff can often pick children up from local schools	Some services (for over 8s) are not required to be registered, although they may be 'quality assured'
Most services are registered and at least half the staff are qualified	Your child cannot attend if he/she is ill
It is unlikely to close due to staff illness	Attending every day may make it difficult for your child to see his/her own friends/have time alone
It gives you one location to drop off your child, and they will be in a familiar place	
Clubs are usually in or near local schools	

Extended Services

Many schools offer a variety of services on top of the normal school day. These range from formal childcare, to activities such as music, art or sport. As a result some schools are open from 8am–6pm, even during school holidays.

Depending on the hours you work, you could opt for a childminder service, or a combination of breakfast clubs (normally open from 8am), after-school clubs (typically open from 3.30–6pm) and holiday play schemes (8am to 6pm during school holidays).

The Working Tax Credit childcare element is available to help with financial support for certain types of school-based care, see page 145.

How do I find an out-of-school service?

- talk to your local Children's Information Service (CIS) to find out more about the out of school services in your area; the **ChildcareLink** freephone service will provide details of your local CIS on 08000 960296 or www.childcarelink.gov.uk

- **4children** can also provide information about school-based care, out-of-school and holiday clubs in your area; visit their website at www.4children.org.uk or call 020 7512 2112.

- in **Scotland**, the **Scottish Out of School Care Network** can provide you with further information; visit www.soscn.org or call 0141 564 1284 or email info@soscn.org

Other sources of information

Your Local Authority will be able to provide information; their contact details can be found in your local phone book. Or ask at your child's school, where they may know of any local services. Finally talk to other parents, who may be able to provide a personal recommendation.

How do I choose the right out-of-school care service for my child and me?

Once you have chosen which type of out-of-school care service you need (depending on whether you work late/start early/need care during the holidays), here are some questions you might want to ask before you decide which service to use:

Questions to ask when choosing your out-of-school service:

- are snacks provided?
- is there an outdoor play area?
- what do the children usually do?
- are there activities such as art, sports or music?
- how are they supervised?
- how much individual attention do they get?
- do they offer homework facilities?
- who is the leader, and what kind of qualifications and experience do they (and other staff) have?
- are the staff trained in first aid?
- is there a separate section for younger children if they can't cope with being in a group of older ones?
- is there an area where children can relax quietly after a day at school if they want?

CHILDCARE FOR DISABLED CHILDREN OR THOSE WITH SPECIAL EDUCATIONAL NEEDS

This chapter explains what support you can expect from childcare providers, it has useful questions you may want to ask when choosing childcare if you have a child with a disability or Special Educational Needs (SEN), and it also has a list of sources of additional information and support.

10

10 CHILDCARE FOR DISABLED CHILDREN OR THOSE WITH SPECIAL EDUCATIONAL NEEDS

The Disability Discrimination Act defines a disabled person as someone who has a mental or physical impairment, which has a substantial and long-term adverse effect on their ability to carry out normal day-to-day activities.

What are Special Educational Needs (SEN)?

Some children have more difficulties than most children of their age with:

- communication
- learning and understanding
- physical and/or sensory development
- behaviour or relating to other people

Children with this type of learning difficulty or disability are said to have "Special Educational Needs" (SEN).

Most out-of-home childcare providers will have a Special Educational Needs Co-ordinator (SENCO), who can discuss with you what is most suitable for you and your child in that setting and who can develop a step-by-step approach to meet your child's individual needs. Your child's needs will usually be met within a nursery, playgroup or school. In some cases an external specialist, such as a speech therapist, may be brought in.

Note that Early Years and childcare providers (such as pre-schools and nurseries) that receive government funding must adhere to the "Special Educational Needs Code of Practice". More details on this can be found at www.direct.gov.uk

Why childcare providers must try to accommodate your child's needs

The Disability Discrimination Acts (1999 and 2005) set out duties to ensure that childcare providers:

- do not discriminate against disabled children
- make "reasonable* adjustments" to include disabled children, and do not treat a disabled child less favourably compared to other children for a reason related to their disability (*What constitutes "reasonable" will depend on the size and resources of the childcare setting)
- provide equal opportunities and be "proactive" in welcoming disabled children

However, regardless of legal obligations, you will naturally want to find a carer to take on your child because they want to, not because they have to.

Choosing Childcare for a Child with a Disability or SEN

Before talking to potential childcare providers, it is important to consider the type of childcare you and your child need, and the childcare they can provide. It is also worth thinking about how you give the childcare provider information about your child. Many people may have pre-conceived or outdated ideas, particularly about specific conditions. It may therefore be more productive to focus on the type of care you are looking for, the nature of activities, personal care, attitude and so on that you expect from the childcarer, rather than the name of the condition. It is important to give detailed information, and to be open about everything that potential carers need to know.

Choosing Specialist Care

Specialist Care
How much does your child need?

Environment
Is it important your child is around other children or is adult attention enough?

CONSIDERATIONS FOR CHOOSING CHILDCARE

Training and Equipment
What does the carer need to support your child?

One-to-One Care
Does your child need it?

Other issues you may want to consider before visiting/interviewing childcare providers are:

- does the carer need to be fit and strong to cope with an older child who needs lifting?
- does your child need to be taken to regular hospital appointments, therapies, or special activities during your working hours?

Questions to ask

In addition to the general questions that apply when looking for childcare (see page 82), below are some other points to bear in mind when looking for childcare for a child with a disability or SEN:

The Care Provider	Do they offer a safe environment for your child, in which they can feel happy and secure?
	Are there appropriate activities according to your child's abilities that they will also enjoy?
	Will their carers treat your child with affection, dignity and respect, without being patronising?
The Staff and Carers	What qualifications and/or training do the staff have, and are they relevant to your child?
	Are they ready and able to provide practical support (for example with personal care)?
	Are carers willing to be shown how to administer medicine? Do they have the relevant insurance?
	Does the carer have the physical capacity to manage your child as well as other children in their care?
The Building	Is the building easy for your child to get around?
	Are physical adaptations needed to the building?
General questions	What equipment is essential? Who will provide it?
	What arrangements can be made in case of an emergency?

COSTS

How much will it cost?

For further information on help with the cost of childcare, see section 3.

In addition, to ensure that you are aware of the full range of benefits to which you are entitled (including Disability Living Allowance) you can call the Disability Benefits Helpline on 0800 88 22 00. They will also be able to advise you on any additional financial support you may be entitled to which will help pay for your childcare.

Where can I find help?

There are many organisations that can help you find the right childcare and necessary support for you and your child. Here are a few examples:

Sure Start Children's Centres

Sure Start is a government programme that aims to deliver the best start in life for every child. Sure Start Children's Centres bring together early education, childcare, heath and family support and are being opened in most disadvantaged areas in England. By 2010, there will be one for every community.

Sure Start Children's Centres have particular commitments to disabled children. Children's Centre professionals should work with you to:

- define the nature of your child's needs and the impact on your family
- look at the support needed and agree the type of the equipment, medical care, therapy, information and practical advice you may need
- agree how, where and when support will be provided

For further information on Sure Start Children's Centres and government Early Years policies, visit the Sure Start website www.surestart.gov.uk or call them on 0870 0002288 for information about how to choose childcare, how to pay for additional support and who to turn to for help.

Childcare providers

You can contact your local authority to find out about Sure Start funding to help with equipment costs, staff training, and adapting facilities and premises such as providing wheelchair access.

Early Support Programme

This is a government initiative to improve services for disabled children and their families, especially those under the age of 3. Programme materials are available free of charge to parents and those who work directly with young children and their families, in England. Early support materials provide:

- information about particular conditions of disabilities which have been identified or 'diagnosed'
- a guide to the 'system' including information about how support services are organised and how to find help
- help in making sense of some of the language that doctors and others use
- signposts to other useful sources of information

The Early Support Family Pack is for families with a child under 3 who need support on a regular basis because their child needs additional help. It is likely to be most useful to families where a range of agencies (such as health, education and social services) are involved and support needs to be well co-ordinated. For an Early Support Family Pack, call the Department for Education and Skills (DfES) publications on 0845 60 222 60 quoting reference ESPP1. For more information, visit www.earlysupport.org.uk

Parent Partnership Services

These provide information, advice and support for parents of children and young people with disabilities and Special Educational Needs. The services are there to help you make informed decisions about your child's education. For further information on Parent Partnership Services, see the Parent Partnership Services on their website www.parentpartnership.org.uk or call DfES Central Correspondence Unit on 0870 0002288.

You can also find your local Parent Partnership Service through your Local Education Authority – visit the website www.dfes.gov.uk/localauthorities/index.cfm or through the National Parent Partnership Network www.parentpartnership.org.uk or call 020 7843 6058.

The DfES has also produced a guide for parents and carers on Special Educational Needs that includes information on what early education settings could do to support your child. Called *Special Educational Needs – A Guide for Parents and Carers*, this is available on the website accompanying this book.

ParentsCentre

This is a website that provides information and support for parents on how to help with your child's learning, including advice on choosing a school and finding childcare. It has dedicated sections on caring for children with disabilities and Special Educational Needs, as well as useful links; visit the website at www.parentscentre.gov.uk

Children's Information Services and ChildcareLink

For further information about childcare and early years services in your area, contact your local Children's Information Service. To find your local service, call 0800 096 02 96 or visit www.childcarelink.gov.uk which will give you information on how to choose childcare, pay for additional support and who to turn to for help.

Local Authority social care services

Your Local Authority can supply information on social care provision for short breaks, Direct Payments, childcare for disabled children, as well as play and leisure services for older disabled children.

You can locate your local social care service providers through your local council. To find your local council go online and visit www.direct.gov.uk or call 0870 0002288.

Voluntary Organisations

There are many charities and voluntary organisations that can help support you and your child in their early development, many of which specialise in supporting children with particular disabilities. On page 135 some of these organisations are listed.

Alternatively, you can go online and visit the website at www.direct.gov. uk/DisabledPeople and click on "Disabled People Contacts", then "learning" for a comprehensive list of relevant voluntary organisations.

Contact a Family

Contact a Family is a UK-wide charity providing advice, information and support to the parents of all disabled children – no matter what their state of health. Contact a Family can also put you in touch with other families with disabled children, both on a local and national basis. You can visit the website for further information at www.cafamily.org.uk or you can call their Helpline 0808 8083555 (Monday–Friday, 10am–4pm) or alternatively email info@cafamily.org.uk.

Parent Support Groups

Getting in touch with these groups can give you the opportunity to meet with other families with young disabled children. You can get practical advice as well as emotional support from parents who are going through the same experiences as you. Charities and voluntary organisations are a good place to start to find support groups in your area. Your local council may also have advice on local groups. To find your local council go online to www.direct.gov.uk or call 0870 0002288.

Working Families

This is an organisation that campaigns for a better work-life balance for families who work and it has a website with details of the support offered on employment rights, childcare and flexible working. Working Families also provides factsheets on childcare for disabled children, as well as guides to the relevant support and employment rights for parents and carers of disabled children.

Factsheet 12: Childcare for Children with Disabilities, is particularly relevant, you can get it on their website at www.workingfamilies.org.uk. It is also available on the website accompanying this book. Alternatively, you can call their freephone Helpline 0800 0130313.

Working Families also has a Special Needs Helpline 020 7253 7243, (Wednesday-Friday, 9.30-1.00 and 2.00-4.30pm).

Crossroads

This is a charity that provides information and access to trained support workers who may be able to come to your home and give you a break from childcare. It has schemes in most parts of England and Wales, which provide a range of services to meet local needs. Many schemes also provide additional services including play schemes for disabled children.

You can use the Scheme Finder on the Crossroads website to locate the nearest Crossroads scheme to you. Visit the website www.crossroads.org.uk or call 0845 4500350.

FINANCIAL SUPPORT FOR WORKING FAMILIES

section
three

section three

FINANCIAL SUPPORT FOR WORKING FAMILIES

This section outlines some of the main benefits and support systems that are in place to help families of working parents financially. It is impossible to summarise the full range of financial support that is available to working families, and to guide you directly to those that you can apply for. Instead, at the beginning of each chapter, you will find a brief description of a benefit or programme followed by information on who can apply for it, and where you can find out more details.

It is important to remember that the amounts available change at least once a year (the financial year runs from 6 April through to 5 April the following year). At the time of going to print, the figures in this book were correct for the financial year 2005 to 2006.

Many of the benefits outlined in this section of the book have restrictions, or there are different rules for non-residents and people who are subject to immigration control. If you are not a UK resident, you live overseas or are subject to immigration control, to clarify if a benefit could apply to you, ask for independent advice from the relevant authority within each section.

In addition to the support outlined in this section, you may also qualify for other financial help such as benefits, loans or grants. If you want to know more, you can find it on the DWP website at www.dwp.gov.uk or go to your local Jobcentre Plus and speak to an adviser there.

TAX CREDITS

If you are working, but your income is low, you may be eligible for Tax Credits to help top up your income. There are two Tax Credits that are available: Child Tax Credit and Working Tax Credit. This chapter explains what these are, who is entitled to claim them and also helps you work out how much you may be entitled to.

11

11 TAX CREDITS

CHILD TAX CREDIT

What is it?

This is a payment made by HM Revenue and Customs (HMRC) to help with the costs of bringing up children. In fact, 90% of all families with children qualify for some Child Tax Credit. You should also read the section in this chapter about Working Tax Credit (see page 143).

Who is it for?

You can claim Child Tax Credit if you are:

- aged 16 years or over and
- responsible for a child under 16 or a young person aged 16 to 20 years who is in full-time non-advanced education or unwaged training, and if they normally live with you (see chapter 12 for details).

Your entitlement to Child Tax Credit will be assessed at the same time as your application for Working Tax Credit. You do not need to claim each tax credit separately.

How is Child Tax Credit calculated?

Child Tax Credit is made up of different elements, which are calculated depending on your personal situation and are added up to find your maximum entitlement. The different elements are:

- **Family Element** (£545) a year, one per family
- **Family Element** (£545) you qualify for this extra amount if you have a baby under a year old
- **Child Element** (£1,765) you qualify for this amount per child
- **Disabled Child Element** (£2,350) you qualify for this for each child or young person who receives Disability Living Allowance or who is registered blind
- **Severely Disabled Child Element** (£945) you qualify for this for each child who receives the highest rate care component of Disability Living Allowance

You are entitled to receive the maximum Child Tax Credit if your income is not more than £14,155 per year. If your income is more than £14,155 per year, your Child Tax Credit entitlement is reduced by 37p for every £1 of income over £14,155 until you are left with just the Family Element of Child Tax Credit (£545). You receive this unless your annual income is £50,000 or more, in which case the Family Element is then reduced by £1 for every £15 of income above £50,000.

Certain income is ignored: for example, all maintenance, Disability Living Allowance, Child Benefit, Guardian's Allowance, benefits for a work-related accident or disease, and £300 a year of income from taxable savings or private pensions.

The ready reckoner overleaf indicates who might qualify for Tax Credits:

Reproduced with permission from Her Majesty's Revenue and Customs. See www.hmrc.gov.uk/taxcredits/reckoner.pdf

A guide to work out your max WTC entitlement

Household Income[2] (£)	Families with children (£s per year)				Families with no children (£s per year)		
	One Child		Two Children		Single	Couple	Single adult with a disability
	No Childcare[1]	Max Childcare[3]	No Childcare	Max Childcare			
0	2,310	2,310	4,080	4,080	0	0	0
5,000	5,620	12,920	7,390	19,905	0	0	3,890
8,000	5,275	12,575	7,045	19,560	1,320	2,960	3,545
10,000	4,535	11,835	6,305	18,820	580	2,220	2,805
15,000	2,685	9,985	4,455	16,970	0	370	955
20,000	835	8,135	2,605	15,120	0	0	0
25,000	545	6,285	755	13,270	0	0	0
30,000	545	4,435	545	11,420	0	0	0
35,000	545	2,585	545	9,570	0	0	0
40,000	545	735	545	7,720	0	0	0
45,000	545	545	545	5,870	0	0	0
50,000	545	545	545	4,020	0	0	0
55,000	210	210	210	2,170	0	0	0
60,000	0	0	0	505	0	0	0

[1] No childcare = not get help or choose to use unregistered childcare

[2] Those with incomes of £5,000 per year are assumed to work part-time (working between 16 and 30 hours a week). In families with £8,000 per year or more, at least 1 adult is assumed to be working 30 or more hours a week.

[3] To qualify for help with childcare costs, you, and your partner if you have one, must work at least 16 hours a week. You will also need to use an approved childcare provider (one who is registered with a local authority or OFDTED). You can receive help towards childcare costs of up to £175 per week for one child, or £300 a week for two or more children.

General Notes: All adults without children or a disability must be between 25 and pension age.

Additional money may also be available for families with a disabled worker or disabled child, a child under 1 year old or someone aged 50 or over returning to work after a period of unemployment.

For example, if you have a household income of £30,000 a year, have two children, and use registered childcare, you may be eligible for up to £11,420 in Tax Credit. This is on top of your income.

Some people receiving Tax Credits may also be able to receive other help

Help available	Who is entitled to claim it?
Free school meals	If you are receiving Child Tax Credit (CTC) only and no Working Tax Credit (WTC) and if your annual income is below £14,155
Health benefits (eg free prescriptions)	If you are receiving WTC or CTC, or WTC with a disability or severe disability element or CTC with no WTC and your income is at or below £15,050
Maternity and Funeral grants	If you are receiving CTC higher than the basic baby or family elements or WTC with disability element
Milk and vitamins	If you are receiving CTC and working less than 16 hours per week and your annual income is at or below £14,155

WORKING TAX CREDIT

What is it?

A payment made by HMRC to people who work for more than 16 hours a week and who are on a low income.

Who is it for?

You may qualify for Working Tax Credit if:

- you and your partner, if you have one, are aged 16 or over, you are working for at least 16 hours a week and you have a low income
- you must also:
    - have a dependant child or
    - have a physical or mental disability which puts you at a

disadvantage in gaining employment and you currently or recently have received benefits for a disability or illness or

- you are aged over 50 and have been on Income Support, Jobseeker's Allowance, Incapacity Benefit or Severe Disablement Allowance

If you do not fit into one of the above categories, you should be aged 25 or over and be working for a minimum of 30 hours a week.

You may also qualify if you are not yet working but will start within 7 days, or if you normally work but you are sick, or on Maternity, Paternity or Adoption leave.

How is Working Tax Credit calculated?

Working Tax Credit is worked out using the same income rules as Child Tax Credit (see page 141).

Working Tax Credit is made up of different elements. These elements are calculated depending on your personal situation and are added up to find your maximum entitlement. The different elements are:

- **Basic element** (£1,665) a year
- **Couple element** (£1,640) – you qualify for this if you have a partner, and are working for at least 30 hours a week; if you are over 50 years old, you will qualify for the 50+ element instead. You may also qualify for the disability element if you work for 16+ hours per week and are registered disabled
- **Lone parent element** (£1,640) – you qualify for this if you are a lone parent
- **30 hour element** (£680) – you qualify for this if you or your partner do paid work for at least 30 hours a week; if you or your partner are responsible for a child or qualifying young person then you are eligible for this element if your combined working time is at least 30 hours a week
- **Disability element** (£2,225) – you qualify for this if you or your partner has a physical or mental disability, which puts either of you at a disadvantage in getting a job (see next page) and you also receive certain benefits for disability or ill-health (if this applies to both of you then you will get two disability elements)

- **Severe disability element** (£945) – you are eligible for this if you get the highest rate of either Disability Living Allowance care component or Attendance Allowance; if you have a partner and you are both severely disabled then you are eligible for two severe disability elements
- **50+ element** – this is paid for one year if you are 50 years or over and have just returned to work after being on benefits; if you are working less than 30 hours you receive £1,140, if you are working 30 hours or more you receive £1,705
- **Childcare element** – the maximum that can be paid is 80% of your childcare costs, up to a weekly limit of £175 for one child and £300 for two or more children, which means that the maximum weekly childcare element you can receive is £140 for one child or £240 for two or more children; but to be eligible, you must use registered or approved childcare (see chapter 7 for more information on what counts as registered childcare)

If you are working and your household income is less than £5,220 a year, you will receive the maximum Working Tax Credit.

For every £1 that you earn above £5,220, you will lose 37p, until you are not entitled to anything.

Disadvantage test for people who are disabled

In order to qualify for the disability element, you must meet one of the 21 criteria on the test. HMRC may ask you to nominate a professional involved in your care who can confirm how your mental or physical disability affects you. For instance, this could be an occupational therapist, a nurse or doctor.

Examples of the criteria include:

- inability to balance unless supported
- registered blind or partially sighted in a register compiled by a local authority
- having difficulty with hearing
- a mental illness for which you receive regular treatment under the supervision of a medically qualified person

Childcare element

If you use **registered childcare**, you can claim the childcare element for any child up to:

- 1 September after their 15th birthday, or
- 1 September after their 16th birthday if the child is on the blind register or came off in the last 28 weeks, or you receive Disability Living Allowance for the child

You must also either be a **lone parent working for at least 16 hours** a week **or if you have a partner**, you are eligible if:

- you both work for at least 16 hours a week or
- one of you works at least 16 hours a week and the other is:
  - an inpatient in hospital
  - in prison
  - incapacitated and receives one of the one of the following benefits:
    - higher, short term rate of Incapacity Benefit (paid after 28 weeks' incapacity for work)
    - Long-term Incapacity Benefit (paid after 52 weeks' incapacity for work)
    - Attendance Allowance
    - Severe Disablement Allowance
    - Disability Living Allowance
    - War Disablement Benefit or Industrial Injuries Attendance Allowance with a Mobility Supplement for you
    - Council Tax Benefit or Housing Benefit with a Disability Premium or Higher Pensioner Premium to you
    - a vehicle under the Invalid Vehicle Scheme

GENERAL INFORMATION ON CLAIMING TAX CREDITS

Claiming your Tax Credits

If you are part of a couple, then you must both make a joint claim for Tax Credits and both of your hours of work, childcare, income and capital are considered jointly. If you separate, each of you must make a new claim.

Generally, your claim for Tax Credits can be backdated for up to 3 months if you were entitled during that time. If you believe that you were entitled during that time, you must ask for your claim to be backdated.

Do Tax Credits affect my other benefits?

If you receive Tax Credits this can affect means-tested benefits. Housing and Council Tax Benefit take account of the Tax Credits you actually receive for Income Support. Child Tax Credit and Child Benefit are ignored for new claims.

It is planned that during late 2006 Child Tax Credit will eventually completely replace all the existing payments for children in families who receive Income Support and Income-Based Jobseeker's Allowance. People who receive payments for children as part of these benefits will be moved onto Child Tax Credit in phases.

What happens if my circumstances change?

Tax Credits are calculated provisionally at the beginning of the claim with a final decision being made at the end of each tax year, when your entitlement and award are compared with your actual income. You are not obliged to tell HMRC if your income changes, but you risk an underpayment or overpayment at the end of the tax year if you do not do so. Remember, if you have been overpaid, you will have to pay the money back (see page 148).

There are some changes in your circumstances which you must inform HMRC about: for example, if you change your employer, someone joins or leaves your family or your childcare costs change by £10 or more a week for more than four weeks. There is a risk of a £300 penalty if you do not tell HMRC.

Overpayments

Overpayments are very likely to happen in a system that uses annual assessments and you must realise that if you are overpaid Tax Credits you may be asked to repay them. This is done automatically by reducing your current Tax Credits in order to adjust the overpayments or by HMRC sending you a bill. Please note that if you receive Income Support, it is not increased to make up for the temporarily reduced Tax Credit.

In law, HMRC has the discretion to waive recovery of any overpayments, however, in practice they can be reluctant to do so. Their policy is to consider not attempting to recover the money in cases where:

- the overpayment has been caused by official error and you could not have reasonably known this
- in cases of hardship

Sometimes HMRC will make "additional payments" to you to ease the effect of an overpayment, but these may eventually have to be repaid at some time.

If you ask for an overpayment to be waived and your request is refused, you can ask for your case to be considered by the Adjudicator. You can also complain to your Member of Parliament and a form of legal action known as judicial review may be possible. You can also ask your MP to refer your complaint to the Parliamentary Ombudsman www.ombudsman.org.uk

FURTHER INFORMATION

- For more information and help, you can call the Tax Credit Helpline on 0845 00 390 or visit the website www.hmrc.gov.uk and click on "Tax Credits".

CHILD BENEFIT

If you are responsible for bringing up a child you may be entitled to receive Child Benefit.

12

12 CHILD BENEFIT

What is it?

Child Benefit is a regular tax-free payment made to people who are bringing up dependant children. It is paid for each child that qualifies and is not affected by income or savings.

Who can claim Child Benefit?

You should claim Child Benefit if you are the person who is the main carer for a dependant child.

To qualify, that child must be:

- under 16
- under 20 and studying in full-time non-advanced education* or on an approved training scheme
  *non-advanced education means attendance at a school, college or similar establishment for education up to and including A-levels, Scottish Certificate of Education (Higher level) or equivalent
- 16 or 17 years old and has left education or training within the last 20 weeks and registered for work or training with the Careers or Connexions Service; they must not be in paid work nor have claimed Income Support, Incapacity Benefit or Jobseeker's Allowance in their own right

If your child spends time in two households, it is not possible to split Child Benefit between different carers. The person who has the main care of the child should claim. If you and another adult share equal care of your child (for example, with their other parent if you are no longer together) you should agree between you who will claim. If you cannot agree and both claim, HMRC will decide who to pay. Where two people in different households share equal care for more than one child, you can each choose to make a claim for a different child.

It is important for the main carer to claim Child Benefit as this may affect your entitlement to other benefits as well as maintenance by the Child Support Agency.

There are special rules about children who are in local authority care, or in hospital for more than 12 weeks or who are in detention. You must seek advice in such cases.

There is no upper age limit on carers who receive Child Benefit.

> **Note:** When you are in work, you usually pay National Insurance Contributions (NICs). This helps your entitlement to other financial support (for example, some other state benefits and your state pension). If you are out of work, you are not paying NICs (unless you qualify for National Insurance credits because you sign on as unemployed or you are sending medical certificates to DWP because you are unable to work due to sickness or disability).
>
> However, if you receive Child Benefit, and if the child is aged under 16 you are entitled to home responsibilities protection. This protects the amount of retirement pension and bereavement benefits you are eligible for if your NICs are affected because you are bringing up children. So, if your partner is working and paying National Insurance, but you are not, then make sure it is you who is claiming the Child Benefit.

How do I claim?

Many parents of new babies receive a "Bounty Pack" in hospital. This may contain a Child Benefit claim form. You must also register the child's birth so that you can claim any benefits or Tax Credits for them. If you did not receive a "Bounty Pack":

- you can order a Child Benefit claim pack by calling the following numbers:
  Great Britain: 0845 302 1444
  Northern Ireland: 0845 603 2000
  Overseas: 0044 191 225 1000
- or you can claim online through the DWP website
  https://esd.dwp.gov.uk/dwp
- the claim form is also available on the website accompanying this book, with guidance notes on how to fill it in. You can download and print out this form, fill it in and post it to the address on the form

You should register the birth and claim as soon as possible after the child is born because Child Benefit can only be backdated for 3 months. If you delay making your claim, you could lose money that you are entitled to.

If you receive a letter or form to say that you do not qualify for Child Benefit, and you believe that this decision is wrong, you can appeal against the decision and ask for your assessment to be done again. The appeal form can be found on the website accompanying this book.

How much money do I receive?

You will get:

- £17.45 per week for the eldest child
- £11.70 per week for each additional child

If you have twins, you will receive the higher amount for the eldest twin only.

If two children in the same family unit qualify, the higher rate is payable only for the eldest child. To give an example, a couple each with a child form a new family unit. Before this they were both receiving higher rate for their eldest child, but now the new family unit is formed, the higher rate is payable only for the eldest child in the new family. This applies regardless of whether each parent continues to claim Child Benefit separately.

Note that 90% of those who are eligible for Child Benefit are also eligible for Child Tax Credit (see page 140).

How is it paid?

Child Benefit is paid every 4 weeks, but it can be paid weekly if:

- you are a single parent
- you – or your partner – are getting Income Support or Income-based Jobseeker's Allowance
- receiving payment every four weeks would cause you hardship

Child Benefit can be paid into your account at:

- banks
- building societies
- post offices
- National Savings accounts

Many banks and building societies will allow you to collect cash from your account at your local Post Office.

For more information visit www.hmrc.gov.uk and click on "Child Benefits".

INCOME SUPPORT AND OTHER BENEFITS

13

13 INCOME SUPPORT AND OTHER BENEFITS

INCOME SUPPORT

If you are only able to work part time and you also have a low wage, then you may be entitled to receive Income Support to top up your earnings.

What is it?

Income Support is a benefit (sum of money) paid to those who have a very low income.

Who is eligible?

You may qualify for Income Support if you fall into one or more of the following categories:

- you are "living in the UK" and have the "right to reside" here
- you are aged between 16 and 60
- you are not in full-time education (though there are exceptions – see below) **and**
- not in paid work for 16 or more hours a week, and, if you have a partner, they must not be working more than 24 hours a week (if you work more than that, you will both not be entitled to Income Support, but you may still qualify for other benefits, such as Tax Credits and/or Housing Benefit)
- the incomes of you and your partner amount to less than the levels set by the government
- you and your partner have less than £16,000 savings/capital (if you have between £6,000 and £16,000 savings/capital, you will be counted as having some income from this)

The rules for Income Support are very complex and the level at which your income qualifies depends on a combination of your family circumstances and the type of income you have.

For example, a lone parent working 10 hours a week who is a tenant, would need to have an income of less than £57.45 a week.

Higher amounts of income are allowed for carers and for people with a disability or long-term illness. If you have a mortgage and/or you are buying a property with service charges (a flat for instance), some of these costs may be added to the level below which your income must be.

When working out your income, certain monies you receive can be ignored, for example, Disability Living Allowance, £10 of any maintenance you receive and, if you receive Child Tax Credit, both this and Child Benefit are not included. A small amount of your earnings is also ignored (between £5 and £20 depending on your circumstances).

It is worthwhile getting advice about this if you think you might qualify for Income Support, because the calculation varies from person to person.

Are there any other reasons why I might be able to claim Income Support?

Here is a list of some of the situations where you could become eligible for Income Support, provided that you also meet the other conditions above:

- you are unable to work because of a disability or illness
- you are entitled to Statutory Sick Pay
- you are regularly and substantially caring for another person and either you receive Carer's Allowance, or one of the following:
    - the person you are caring for is receiving Attendance Allowance
    - the middle or higher rate of Disability Living Allowance care component
    - the constant attendance allowance paid under the Industrial Disablement Benefit or War Disablement Pension rules
- you are caring for another person who has applied for one of the above benefits, but their claim has not yet been decided – you will be able to claim Income Support for up to 26 weeks while you are waiting for a decision
- you are a lone parent and responsible for a child aged under 16 years
- you or your partner are expecting a baby (you are eligible from 11 weeks before the baby is expected until 15 weeks after it is born)
- the pregnancy means that you are too ill to work

These are just some of the situations that may arise – there are many more and you should get advice to find out whether or not your circumstances fit into any of them.

What must I do to claim Income Support?

When you claim Income Support, you are usually asked to attend a Work Focused Interview. If you do not attend this interview without good reason, your claim will not succeed, though you can appeal against this. An interview can be waived (abandoned) or put off until later if it would not be helpful or it is not appropriate in your circumstances.

If you do receive Income Support, this means that you will also qualify for free school meals, free prescriptions, maximum help with your rent and Council Tax.

HOUSING AND COUNCIL TAX BENEFITS

If you receive Income Support or income-based Jobseeker's Allowance, you will be "passported" or put onto the maximum levels of these. However, it is possible to receive Housing and Council Tax Benefits even if you are in full-time work if you are on a low wage.

To qualify for Housing Benefit you and any partner must:

- be living and have a right to reside in the UK
- be liable for rent or other payments for your accommodation (but note that mortgage and leasehold service charges do not qualify)
- if you rent from a close relative, the payments agreement must be commercial and you must not live with them

To qualify for Council Tax Benefit you and any partner must:

- be required to pay Council Tax **and**
- have less than £16,000 in capital and/or savings (if you have between £6,000 and £16,000, you will be counted as having some income from this) **and**
- have a low enough income

There are no set levels below which your income must fall, because your entitlement depends on your family and household circumstances, your income and your rent/Council Tax level.

You can live in the home that you own and still qualify for Council Tax Benefit.

If you rent from a private landlord (not a Registered Housing Association), the maximum amount of rent for which you may receive help may be less than the amount you have to pay. Sometimes, if you have an adult non-dependent living in your home, this can affect the amount of Housing Benefit you qualify for.

How do I work out if my income is low enough?

Here are some examples of maximum incomes that you can earn and still qualify for Housing Benefit. Please note that these are only rough guides, so you should ask advice to check whether or not you do qualify.

When working out your income, Tax Credits count as income, but some types of income are ignored - for example, Child Benefit, Disability Living Allowance and £10 a week of any maintenance you receive.

A couple with 2 children working 30 hours a week: Housing Benefit

Weekly rent	Maximum weekly income to qualify for Housing Benefit
£60	£136
£75	£337
£100	£375
£120	£406
£140	£437
£200	£529

A couple with 2 children working 30 hours a week: Council Tax Benefit

Annual Council Tax	Maximum weekly income to qualify for Council Tax Benefit
£800	£299
£1200	£338
£1600	£376
£2000	£415

A lone parent working 16 hours a week with 1 child: Housing Benefit

Weekly rent	Maximum weekly income to qualify for Housing Benefit
£60	£251
£75	£274
£100	£312
£120	£343
£140	£374
£200	£466

A lone parent working 16 hours a week with 1 child: Council Tax Benefit

Annual Council Tax	Maximum weekly income to qualify for Council Tax Benefit
£800	£236
£1200	£275
£1600	£313
£2000	£351

Some people who have higher incomes can still qualify, for example, carers and people with a disability and also some people who have childcare costs.

If your income and capital is otherwise too high for Council Tax Benefit, you may qualify for a type of Council Tax Benefit known as a "Second Adult Rebate" if you have an adult living in your home whose weekly income is less than £204. They must not be your partner or a lodger or sub-tenant, but could be someone such as an adult son or daughter, a parent or a friend who is on a low income.

CHILDCARE VOUCHERS

If you are working and using registered childcare, then you may be able to save some money on the cost of your childcare by using Childcare Vouchers.

14

14 CHILDCARE VOUCHERS

KEY FACTS

Each working parent:

- Can claim up to £55 a week free of tax and National Insurance.
- Must use Childcare Vouchers with registered or approved childcare.
- Must use childcare providers who are members of the Childcare Voucher scheme.

What are they?

Childcare Vouchers are issued by your employer and are designed to help working parents with the cost of childcare. You will normally receive them instead of your salary (this *may* have an effect on your entitlement to help with childcare costs through Tax Credits, (see Salary Sacrifice, page 181). If your firm does offer this, they normally run a scheme with the help of a Childcare Voucher company. Not all employers offer their staff this scheme.

The benefit of Childcare Vouchers is that **they allow you to claim up to £55 a week free of tax and National Insurance** (see 'How much are they?' on page 163 for more information).

Your voucher will look like this

Who are they for?

- Childcare Vouchers are available to anyone regardless of income but note that this does not apply to self-employed people
- Vouchers can be issued either for your child or for a stepchild who lives with you (full-time or part-time), or for a child whom you provide maintenance for. Vouchers can also be issued for a child who is not related to you but who is living with you, and for whom you are providing parental responsibility (see page 8 for information on parental responsibility)
- Childcare Vouchers can be claimed for your child up to:
  - – 1 September after the child's 15th birthday or
  - – 1 September following their 16th birthday if the child is disabled

Where do I get them from?

- Childcare Vouchers are issued by employers but not all employers offer them
- if your employer does offer the scheme, it must be available to all employees in your company or location; employers are not allowed to offer Childcare Vouchers only to specific staff (there can be no discrimination on the grounds of gender, seniority or position, level of pay or length of service)

For information on help with childcare costs via Tax Credits, see chapter 11.

How much are they worth?

You can choose to receive any amount in Childcare Vouchers. The first £55 a week is free from tax and National Insurance Contributions, which helps you save money.

This means that a basic-rate taxpayer[1] can save up to £916 per year, and a higher-rate taxpayer can save up to £1,195 per year. Each employed parent can claim Childcare Vouchers, so a 2-parent family could save up to £1,832 (basic tax rate) or £2,390 (higher tax rate).

Regardless of how many children you have, only the first £55 a week is free from tax and NI contributions.

1   If you earn between £0 and £2,150 you pay 10% starting rate tax. Between £2,151 and £33,300 you pay 22% basic rate tax. If you earn over £33,300 a year, you pay a higher rate tax of 40%.

The table below indicates the maximum amount you can save by choosing to receive Childcare Vouchers.

	One-parent family		Two-parent family	
	Basic tax payer	Higher rate tax payer	Basic tax payer	Higher rate tax payer
Weekly	£17.62	£22.98	£35.23	£45.96
Monthly	£76.33	£99.58	£152.67	£199.17
Annually	£916	£1,195	£1,832	£2,390

Where can I use them?

Any childcare provider can accept Childcare Vouchers as long as they have a bank account. The childcare provider will claim the value of the voucher from the Childcare Voucher company, usually by direct payment into their bank account. There is no cost to the childcare provider in receiving payment through Childcare Vouchers.

To qualify for tax and National Insurance exemptions, the childcare must be registered or approved. See pages 85-87 for further information on what is meant by registered or approved childcare.

If I already have childcare, can I start using Childcare Vouchers?

- If you already use a registered childcarer, such as a nanny, and want to take advantage of the benefits offered by Childcare Vouchers, your childcare provider must join the Childcare Voucher Scheme.
- Childcare providers can join the scheme by registering at www.childcarevouchers.co.uk
- The voucher company will send the vouchers, personalised with your employer details, and your personal details. The vouchers can be sent as frequently as required either to your employer or direct to your home.
- You use the voucher to pay your childcare provider, who then sends them back to the voucher provider for payment.
- The childcare provider usually receives payment within one working day of the voucher company receiving the vouchers.

Can I use Childcare Vouchers if I use a workplace nursery or crèche?

Yes. If you use childcare facilities at a workplace premises, even if you work for another employer on the premises, the same tax and National Insurance exemptions will apply.

How do I get them?

There are 2 different ways in which Childcare Vouchers can be offered:

- as a straight benefit
- as part of a Salary Sacrifice Scheme

As a straight benefit Your employer may offer you Childcare Vouchers as a benefit in addition to your salary.

As a Salary Sacrifice Scheme This is where a parent elects to take a reduction of their salary, and instead receives that amount in Childcare Vouchers. Being offered Childcare Vouchers in replacement for Salary Sacrifice is the most common option. The only legal consideration is that your cash pay must not fall below the National Minimum Wage (see page 183). For more details on Salary Sacrifice see chapter 17.

How does it work?

When you sign up to a Childcare Voucher Salary Sacrifice Scheme you will generally be required to do so for a fixed period of time (often 1 year), after which your agreement can be reviewed. You will be asked to sign a contract confirming that you agree to exchange part of your salary for Childcare Vouchers. This means that (within the period covered by the agreement) you will not be able to stop receiving Childcare Vouchers and revert back to receiving your full salary. Most schemes/employers will offer an earlier review of your agreement in the event of an unexpected life change, which means anything linked to birth, death and marriage. In other extreme circumstances your employer can ask their local Tax Office if you may leave the Scheme but it is best to discuss this with your employer prior to signing an agreement.

For details of how the payment of Childcare Vouchers may affect other benefits you are receiving, talk to your personal adviser at the Jobcentre Plus.

CHILD TRUST FUND

A Child Trust Fund is a way to help you and your child to save for the future. The Government gives a sum of money which you invest for your child. After the age of 18 your child can spend the money on whatever they want, such as driving lessons, university fees or a deposit on a property.

15

15 CHILD TRUST FUND

KEY FACTS

- It enables you to open a long-term savings and investment account from which your child (and no-one else) can withdraw the money when they reach 18.
- You will receive a £250 voucher to start each child's account.
- Money cannot be taken out of the CTF once it has been put in – when your child is 18 years old they will be able to decide how to use the money.
- Children in families receiving Child Tax Credit (CTC), with a household income that qualifies for the maximum amount of CTC, will receive a higher amount.
- Your child will not pay tax on income and gains in the account.
- Up to a maximum of £1,200 each year can be saved in the account by parents, family or friends.
- The government will make a further contribution when your child is aged 7 years.
- You can choose the type of account you wish to open: cash, shares or stakeholder.
- The CTF will not affect any benefits or Tax Credits you or your child receives.

What is the Child Trust Fund?

- the Child Trust Fund (CTF) is a savings and investment account provided for each child in the UK born on or after 1 September 2002, provided that the child qualifies for Child Benefit
- the government contributes to the account of every child
- the CTF does not operate like a traditional savings account – no money paid into the CTF can be drawn out until at least the child's 18th birthday
- the account and the money belong to the child when they are 18 years old, and they are free to spend it as they wish
- the Child Trust Fund won't affect your own or your child's entitlement to benefits and Tax Credits

How much is it worth?

At least £500 For children born on or after 6 April 2005, the government provides an initial £250. For children born between 1 September 2002 and 5 April 2005, the voucher will have a higher value, recognising that, for these children, there will be less time for the CTF to grow in value.

The table below outlines the amount the initial voucher will be worth, depending on when your child was born.

Child's birthday	Amount received
On or after 6 April 2005	£250
6 April 2004 – 5 April 2005	£256
6 April 2003 – 5 April 2004	£268
1 September 2002 – 5 April 2003	£277
Born before 1 September 2002	£0

The account must be opened with a government-approved Child Trust Fund provider. A list of all the approved providers can be found on page 172, or visit the CTF website www.childtrustfund.gov.uk

Children in families that receive Child Tax Credit AND have an annual income at or below the income limit (£14,310 in 2006–7) will be paid an extra £250 in addition to the starting contribution of £250. That makes a total initial investment of £500.

When your child reaches 7 years old, he/she will receive a further £250 to put into their account.

Your account provider will give you an annual statement so that you can keep track of the value of the fund.

How do I get it?

Every child born on or after 1 September 2002 is eligible for the CTF.

Follow the flowchart on the following page to see if your child is eligible.

In order to receive your voucher:

- you must be receiving Child Benefit (see chapter 12)
  - the child must be living in the United Kingdom and
  - they must not not subject to immigration control

The children of Crown Servants (including the Armed Forces) posted abroad qualify because they are treated as living in the UK.

A Child Trust Fund Account can only be opened with the voucher provided. There is one voucher for every child and they are sent out through the post to the person who claims Child Benefit for the child.

If you believe your child qualifies for a CTF but you have not received your voucher, you can call the Child Trust Fund Helpline on 0845 302 1470.

Where can I cash the voucher?

There are 3 different types of Trust Fund. It is up to you to choose the type of Trust Fund that suits your needs and the level of risk you are happy to take (see table on page 171).

IS MY CHILD ELIGIBLE ?

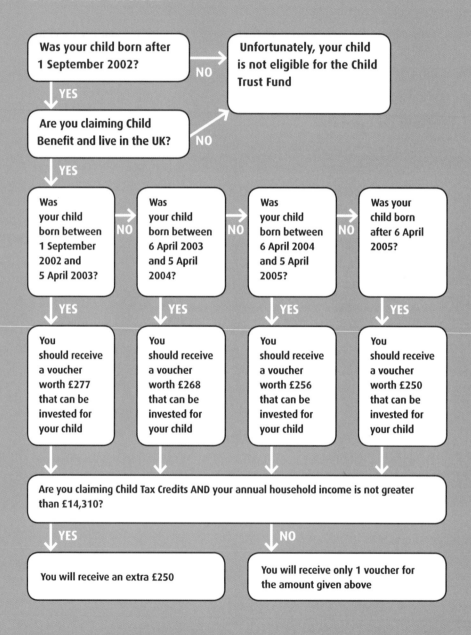

Was your child born after 1 September 2002?

NO →

Unfortunately, your child is not eligible for the Child Trust Fund

YES ↓

Are you claiming Child Benefit and live in the UK?

NO →

YES ↓

Was your child born between 1 September 2002 and 5 April 2003?

NO →

Was your child born between 6 April 2003 and 5 April 2004?

NO →

Was your child born between 6 April 2004 and 5 April 2005?

NO →

Was your child born after 6 April 2005?

YES ↓

You should receive a voucher worth £277 that can be invested for your child

YES ↓

You should receive a voucher worth £268 that can be invested for your child

YES ↓

You should receive a voucher worth £256 that can be invested for your child

YES ↓

You should receive a voucher worth £250 that can be invested for your child

Are you claiming Child Tax Credits AND your annual household income is not greater than £14,310?

YES ↓

You will receive an extra £250

NO ↓

You will receive only 1 voucher for the amount given above

There are 3 types of Trust Funds:
Savings Accounts (low risk, potential low returns)
This is the basic kind of CTF and is the most secure. Your child will get back the value of their voucher, plus any interest earned. While this is the most secure CTF, it also means that it is less likely to grow as much as an account invested in shares.
Shares (high risk, potential high returns)
This account carries more risk than a basic savings account as the money is invested in stocks and shares. However, the potential growth of the fund is higher.
Stakeholder (medium risk, potentially medium returns)
This account starts as a shares account but automatically moves to a lower risk saving account when the child reaches the age of 13.

Once you have chosen the type of fund you wish to open, you can contact any of the providers listed in the table on page 172, which offer Child Trust Fund accounts. If the account is not opened within 1 year of the voucher being sent, HM Revenue and Customs will automatically open a stakeholder account for your child.

The Child Trust Fund website has a calculator that can estimate potential growth of the account at www.childtrustfund.gov.uk

Providers of Child Trust Funds

Name of Child Trust Fund Provider	Phone number	Website address	Saving	Shares	Stake-holder
4thekids	020 7499 9097	www.4thekids.co.uk		x	x
Abbey	0800 302030	www.abbey.com	x		x
Ancient Order of Foresters Friendly Society	08000 898980	www.teddytrust.co.uk		x	x
Britannia Building Society	0845 121 7909	www.britannia.co.uk	x		x
Child Trust Fund.com	0800 028 0040	www.childtrustfund.com			x
The Children's Mutual	0845 077 1899	www.thechildrensmutual.co.uk		x	x
The Chorley & District Building Society	01257 419 105	www.chorleybs.co.uk	x		x
Druids Sheffield Friendly Society	01709 876 409	www.druidsfriendly.co.uk	x		x
F & C Management Ltd	0800 136420	www.fandc.com		x	x
Family Investments	0800 616 695	www.familyinvestments.co.uk			x
Foresters	0800 990022	www.foresters.co.uk			x
Furness Building Society	0800 220568	www.furnessbs.co.uk	x		x
Halifax Financial Services	0845 609 0064	www.halifax.co.uk			x

Providers of Child Trust Funds continued

Name of Child Trust Fund Provider	Phone number	Website address	Saving	Shares	Stake-holder
Hanley Economic Building Society	01782 255 000	www.thehanley.co.uk	x		x
HSBC	0800 520420	www.hsbc.co.uk			x
Ipswich Building Society	0845 230 8686	www.ipswichbuildingsociety.co.uk	x		x
Killik & co	020 7337 0400	www.killik.co.uk		x	x
Kingston Unity Friendly Society	0113 245 7131	www.kingstonunity.co.uk		x	x
Leeds Building Society	0113 225 7777	www.leedsbuildingsociety.co.uk	x		x
Leeds City Credit Union Ltd	0113 214 5252	www.leedscitycreditunion.co.uk	x		x
Liverpool Victoria	0800 085 8811	www.liverpoolvictoria.co.uk	x		x
Mercantile Building Society	0191 295 9500	www.mercantile-bs.co.uk	x		x
Methodist Chapel Aid Limited	01904 622 150	www.methodistchapel.co.uk	x		x
Monmouthshire Building Society	01633 844 444	www.monbsoc.co.uk	x		x
NatWest	0845 603 0313	www.natwest.com			x
Nationwide Building Society	0800 302010	www.nationwide.co.uk	x		x
Pilling & Co	0161 819 4850	www.pilling.co.uk		x	x
Police Mutual Assurance Society	0800 652 9327	www.pmas.co.uk		x	x
Redmayne-Bentley Stockbrokers	0113 200 6560	www.redmayne.co.uk	x		x

Providers of Child Trust Funds continued

Name of Child Trust Fund Provider	Phone number	Website address	Saving	Shares	Stake-holder
Royal Bank of Scotland	0845 604 4500	www.RBS.co.uk			X
Schoolteachers Friendly Society	0151 724 1930	www.schoolteachers.org.uk			X
Scottish Friendly Asset Managers	0800 585 625	www.scottishfriendly.co.uk			X
Selftrade	0845 0700 720	www.selftrade.co.uk		X	X
The Share Centre	0800 800 008	www.share.com		X	X
Skipton Building Society	08457 171 777	www.skipton.co.uk	X		X
Ulster Bank Limited	0845 601 0120	www.Ulsterbank.com			X
Walker Crips Stockbrokers Limited	020 7253 7502	www.wcwb.co.uk		X	X
Yorkshire Building Society	0845 1200 100	www.ybs.co.uk	X		X

Can I pay extra money into the account?

Yes, you, your family, friends and the even the child are allowed to pay additional money into the account, up to £1,200 per year per child. Although the account is tax-free, there is no tax relief on the money that is paid into the account.

Step-by-step guide to starting your Child Trust Fund Account

Step 1: Claim Child Benefit (see chapter 12)

You must apply for and be awarded Child Benefit before you can open an account. Shortly after you have been awarded Child Benefit, you will automatically receive a CTF information pack and a voucher for £250 for your child.

Step 2: Decide which type of account suits you best

Decide if you would like to open a savings account, a shares account or a stakeholder account (see the table on page 171).

Step 3: Choose a Child Trust Fund Account Provider and open an account

The table on pages 172-4 lists all current account providers. You will also find a list of account providers in the information pack you will be sent, or on the Child Trust Fund website at www.childtrustfund.gov.uk Contact the provider directly. You will need your voucher to open the account.

For further information on choosing and opening a CTF account, you can visit the Child Trust Fund website designed to help you at www.ctfhelp.com or call the helpline on 0845 302 1470.

SUMMARY

1: Claim Child Benefit for your child
- once this has been awarded, you will automatically receive information on CTF and then a voucher

→ the Voucher represents money from the government, and a CTF cannot be set up without one

→ if you previously claimed Child Benefit but no longer do, you will still automatically receive the voucher

2: Set up a CTF account for your child
- there are 3 steps in this process

STEP 1 Choose which TYPE OF ACCOUNT
- there are 3 types of account to choose from

→ Savings account

→ Stakeholder account

→ Share investment account

STEP 2 Choose a PROVIDER
- this is a financial institution such as a bank or building society (shop around before you decide)

→ for a full up-to-date list of providers see the table on pages 172-4 or go to www.childtrustfund.gov.uk

STEP 3 Open the Account
- all you need to do is take your voucher to your chosen provider, or post it if you open the account online or by phone

→ you may need to take proof of your identity with you – check with the provide

→ make a note of the unique reference number on the voucher – it may be useful for future enquiries

3: Your child's CTF account is now set up
- you remain the legal contact for the account until your child is 16.
- at 18 your child may withdraw the money
- the provider will pass on the details of your voucher to HMRC, who will credit that amount to your child's new account

→ check annual statements from the provider to make sure you are happy with the growth of your child's money

→ you can move the CTF account if you are not happy with its performance

→ you, your family and friends may pay in up to a maximum of £1,200 per year

SURE START MATERNITY GRANT

If you are on a low income, and are expecting or already have a new baby, you may be able to apply for a Sure Start Maternity Grant to help you purchase some of the extra things you need.

16

16 SURE START MATERNITY GRANT

What is it?

It is a sum of £500 that you are given for your child, which is intended to help you buy the things you will need for your new baby, such as nappies, clothes and equipment.

Who can claim it?

You are eligible to receive the Sure Start Maternity Grant if you can say "yes" to a question in column A **and** "yes' to a question in column B in the table on the opposite page.

Eligibility Chart

A		B
Have you been awarded any of the following:		Have you and/or your partner/ spouse:
Income Support or income-based Jobseeker's Allowance?		become pregnant and are within 11 weeks of giving birth?
Working Tax Credit with a disability or severe disability element?		given birth in the last three months?
Child Tax Credit which is paid at more than the family element of £545 a year, or £1,090 if you have a baby under 1 year old?	**AND**	adopted a child under the age of 1 in certain circumstances or have a Residence Order for such a child? (if so, you must claim within 3 months of the order being made)
Pension Credit?		been granted a parental order for a child born to a surrogate mother? (if so, you must claim within 3 months of the order being made)

If you claim before the baby is born, you must also have received advice on the health of the baby and your health from a healthcare professional.

If you have applied for other benefits or Tax Credits and are waiting to hear if your application has been successful, do not delay in making your claim for a Sure Start Maternity Grant because you must apply within 3 months of the birth of your baby.

CAN I CLAIM A SURE START MATERNITY GRANT?

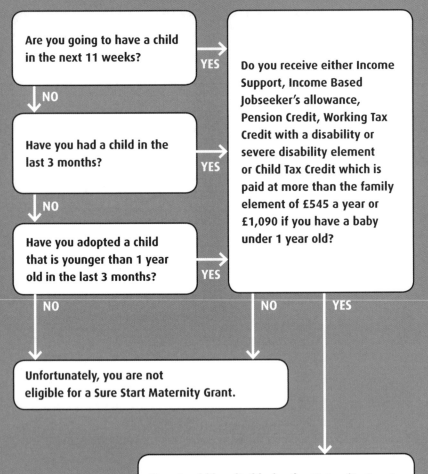

Are you going to have a child in the next 11 weeks?

NO

Have you had a child in the last 3 months?

NO

Have you adopted a child that is younger than 1 year old in the last 3 months?

NO

YES

YES

YES

Do you receive either Income Support, Income Based Jobseeker's allowance, Pension Credit, Working Tax Credit with a disability or severe disability element or Child Tax Credit which is paid at more than the family element of £545 a year or £1,090 if you have a baby under 1 year old?

NO

YES

Unfortunately, you are not eligible for a Sure Start Maternity Grant.

You should be eligible for the Maternity Grant of up to £500. You will need to fill in the SF100 form which you can get at Jobcentre Plus, Social Security Offices, Benefit Agencies or DWP websites. This form is also available on the website accompanying this book.

SALARY SACRIFICE SCHEME

You may be able to exchange some of your wages for other benefits, enabling you to get them free from income and National Insurance.

17

17 SALARY SACRIFICE SCHEME

What is Salary Sacrifice?

Salary Sacrifice is the term used to describe what happens when you formally agree to give up part of your cash salary in exchange for a non-cash item or service, such as in return for Childcare Vouchers.

When you accept a job offer, there is usually an employment package and this can include:

- cash wages or salary
- certain benefits (for example a company car or medical insurance)

If you and your employer agree to reduce the amount of wages you get and replace it with a benefit, this is called Salary Sacrifice.

What is the benefit?

Depending on what the Salary Sacrifice is being made for, some benefits may give you tax and National Insurance exemptions. For example, you may agree to a reduction in wages of £55 a week in exchange for Childcare Vouchers. Childcare Vouchers are exempt from tax and National Insurance payments (see page 163 for more details).

What should I consider before entering into a Salary Sacrifice arrangement?

It is essential to understand what the sacrifice will mean in practical terms. You should consider carefully the effect, or potential effect, that a reduction in your pay might have on:

- your **future right to your original salary** (before the sacrifice)

- your **entitlement to Working Tax Credit or Child Tax Credit** – for example, if you sacrifice your salary for childcare costs, you will qualify for less help towards your childcare costs from Tax Credits (for information about childcare costs and Tax Credits, see page 139)
- any **entitlement to State Pension or other benefits** such as Statutory Maternity Pay – for example, if your salary is reduced to less than the level where you have to pay National Insurance contributions
- any **employer's pension scheme** being contributed to – for instance, a Salary Sacrifice may mean that you will be paying less into the scheme and this may have an effect on your final pension entitlement

A Salary Sacrifice should not reduce your cash wage to below the **National Minimum Wage**. The table below tells you what the minimum wage is depending on your age:

22+ years	18–21 years	16–17 years
The main rate for workers aged 22 or over is currently set at £5.05 an hour	The development rate for 18–21-year-olds is currently set at £4.25 an hour	The development rate for 16–17 year olds is currently set at £3.00 an hour
On 1 October 2006, this increases to £5.35	On 1 October 2006, this increases to £4.45	On 1 October 2006, this increases to £3.30 an hour

When is Salary Sacrifice effective?

Salary sacrifice arrangements are effective when the contractual right to cash pay has been reduced. For that to happen, 2 conditions have to be met:

- the potential future pay must be given up before it is treated as received for tax or NICs purposes
- the revised contractual arrangement between employer and employee must be that the employee is entitled to lower cash pay and a benefit

WILL I BENEFIT FROM SALARY SACRIFICE?

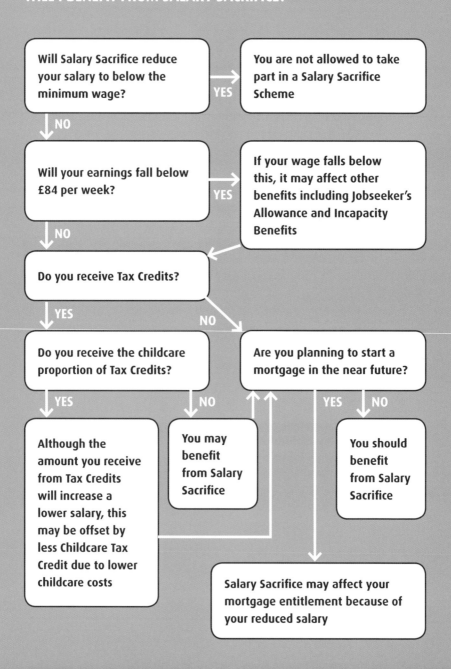

Will Salary Sacrifice reduce your salary to below the minimum wage?

→ YES → **You are not allowed to take part in a Salary Sacrifice Scheme**

NO ↓

Will your earnings fall below £84 per week?

→ YES → **If your wage falls below this, it may affect other benefits including Jobseeker's Allowance and Incapacity Benefits**

NO ↓

Do you receive Tax Credits?

YES ↓   NO →

Do you receive the childcare proportion of Tax Credits?

Are you planning to start a mortgage in the near future?

YES ↓   NO ↓   YES ↓   NO ↓

Although the amount you receive from Tax Credits will increase a lower salary, this may be offset by less Childcare Tax Credit due to lower childcare costs

You may benefit from Salary Sacrifice

You should benefit from Salary Sacrifice

Salary Sacrifice may affect your mortgage entitlement because of your reduced salary

HOW OTHER STATE BENEFITS ARE AFFECTED

Will Salary Sacrifice affect my state pension or other benefits?

Yes. A Salary Sacrifice may affect your entitlement to state benefits and Tax Credits.

When you sacrifice cash in return for a benefit that is free from National Insurance Contributions (NICs), such as Childcare Vouchers, you save on the NICs and will get more vouchers for your money. However, be aware that it also:

- reduces your earnings on which you pay NICs
- may take your earnings below £84 a week, for which NICs are due

Your entitlement to some benefits is based on the amount of NICs that you pay, and others on your earnings. Entering into a Salary Sacrifice Scheme may therefore affect your current or future entitlement to a range of benefits.

For most employees, paying less NICs may not adversely affect your benefit entitlement because:

- you may still be paying enough NICs to qualify for benefits
- you may already be earning below £84 a week (the minimum you need to earn before you pay NICs)
- if you only participate in Salary Sacrifice for a short period, your contributions will only be affected for that period, which therefore has a minimal affect on your benefit entitlement

How Contribution-based benefits are affected

Incapacity Benefit (IB)

If your earnings fall below £84 a week, you may not be entitled to IB. If this happens, you may be entitled to Income Support (see page 154).

Jobseeker's Allowance (JSA)

If your earnings fall below £84 a week, you may not be entitled to JSA (contribution-based). If you have not paid enough NICs, you will lose entitlement to this benefit. You may still be able to claim JSA (income-based).

State pension

If you have not paid enough NICs on your income, you may have a reduced or no State Pension when you retire.

How earnings-related benefits are affected

Maternity Allowance (MA)

If your earnings fall below £30 a week (on average) then you will lose your entitlement to MA. If your earnings are between £30 and £115, then you will receive a reduced amount. If your average earnings are more than £115 a week, then you will receive the full standard amount of MA.

Work-related payments

Statutory Maternity Pay (SMP)

If your average weekly earnings fall below £84 a week, you will lose your entitlement to SMP. If this happens, you may still be entitled to Maternity Allowance. If you are still entitled to SMP, the higher rate, which you receive for the first 6 weeks, will be reduced as it is based on your cash earnings.

Statutory Sick Pay (SSP)

If your average weekly earnings fall below £84 a week, you will lose your right to SSP. If this happens, then you may still be entitled to Income Support based on incapacity, or Incapacity Benefit.

Working Tax Credit (WTC)

The amount of WTC you receive depends on several factors, such as the number of hours you work, how many children you have and whether you use registered or approved childcare.

A Salary Sacrifice for Childcare Vouchers or the provision of an employer – provided nursery place can reduce your relevant pay for Tax Credit purposes because the value of these benefits is not calculated as income. This may increase the amount of WTC you receive.

If you are eligible to receive the childcare element of WTC, the costs eligible for the childcare element will be reduced by the Childcare Voucher, which would mean that the amount of your childcare element of WTC would be reduced.

You need to consider whether it is worth claiming Tax Credits before you enter into a Salary Sacrifice arrangement and what the effect on your Tax Credits might be.

Employers

The "sacrifice" is achieved by varying the employee's terms and conditions of employment relating to pay. Salary Sacrifice is a matter of employment law, not tax law. Where an employee agrees to a Salary Sacrifice in return for a non-cash benefit, they give up their contractual right to future cash remuneration. Employers and employees who are thinking of entering into such arrangements are advised to obtain legal advice on whether their proposed arrangements will achieve their desired result.

FURTHER INFORMATION

- Contact the Department for Work and Pensions or your local Jobcentre Plus office.

- For enquiries about pensions, you can visit the Pension Service website www.thepensionservice.gov.uk

- For enquiries about the impact of a Salary Sacrifice arrangement on other benefits, contact your local Jobcentre Plus office, or visit their website: www.jobcentreplus.gov.uk or call DWP on 020 7712 2171.

GUARDIAN'S ALLOWANCE

If you are looking after a child that may not be yours, you may be entitled to receive Guardian's Allowance to help you with some of the financial costs.

18

18 GUARDIAN'S ALLOWANCE

What is it?

Guardian's Allowance is paid to help with the cost of bringing up children after the death of one parent or both parents or where, in certain circumstances, the parents are unable to care for their child.

It is also available for carers of children if one parent has died and the other is:

- separated or divorced (certain conditions apply)
- in prison (for 2 years or more)
- detained in hospital under court order
- untraceable

Who can claim it?

You can claim this if you are seen as responsible for a child you live with and/or contribute towards the cost of providing for them.

The child must be:

- under 16 years of age
- aged 16 or 17 years old, have left education or training within the last 20 weeks and have registered for work or training with the Careers or Connexions Services. They must not be in paid work or have claimed Income Support, Incapacity Benefit or Jobseeker's Allowance themselves
- under 20 years old and studying in full-time non-advanced education* or an approved training scheme
  *non-advanced education means attendance at a school, college or similar establishment for education up to and including GCSEs, A-levels, Scottish Certificate of Education (Higher level) or equivalent

You do not need to be a legal guardian to claim Guardian's Allowance.

You must also qualify for Child Benefit (see chapter 12).

How much is it?

You are paid £12.50 per week for each child.

Guardian's Allowance is not treated as income and is paid in addition to Tax Credits and benefits.

How do I claim it?

You can get an application pack and instruction booklet by calling the Guardian's Allowance Unit on 0845 302 1464. Or you can visit the HM Revenue and Customs website to download the form and instruction booklet at www.hmrc.gov.uk

The application forms are also available on the website accompanying this book.

THE ENTERPRISE NURSERY SCHEME

If you are working, then you may be able to save money on your childcare by making an agreement with your employer that will take advantage of tax breaks.

19

19 THE ENTERPRISE NURSERY SCHEME

What is it?

The Enterprise Nursery Scheme is a network of privately owned nurseries run by a management company called TEDS Management.

Employers can pay the nursery fees directly out of your salary, before you are subject to income tax or National Insurance.

Where can I use it?

TEDS Management Ltd is a leading provider of Workplace Nurseries in the United Kingdom and it has a network of more than 300 nurseries across the UK. If, however, you want to use a nursery that is not currently a member of the scheme, then TEDS would approach them to see if they want to join.

How much money would I save?

You would save your tax and National Insurance on the money paid to the nursery.

For example, if you are a basic rate taxpayer (see page 197) and you are spending £6,500 a year on nursery fees, you will save £1,985.82 annually, that is £165.48 a month.

If you are a higher rate taxpayer, and pay £10,000 on childcare, you would save £4,200 a year, that is £350 a month.

The advantages for you are:
- childcare fees are reduced immediately
- it's easy to sign up
- if you move jobs you can transfer the scheme from employer to employer
- you can choose the nursery that best suits your needs
- you can transfer from nursery to nursery

The advantages to an employer are:
- employees are able to benefit from quality childcare at a reduced cost
- this attractive benefit aids retention of trained and skilled staff
- there are no additional costs to the employer
- management of nursery provision is outsourced
- the scheme is open to both mothers and fathers
- although you need to pay TEDS Management a fee for providing management services, this comes out of the employer National Insurance savings, and is therefore not an additional cost

Advantages for the nursery are:
- parents using the nursery benefit from a substantial cost saving but it does not mean the nursery has to lower its standards or reduce its profit margins
- the scheme offers the nursery an extra competitive edge ahead of other nurseries in the area
- the nursery can receive a financial benefit for every child using the scheme

How do I join?
You can complete a form on-line – visit their website at www.teds.uk.com

Alternatively, call them on 0845 345 8662 and they will send you an information pack.

RETURNING TO EDUCATION OR TRAINING

section four

RETURNING TO EDUCATION OR TRAINING

Are you a parent who has had time off work to look after and bring up your children and as a result, have not worked for 2, 3, 4 or 5 years or possibly longer? Or perhaps you have never worked before but are now ready to find employment? Perhaps you want to find a better job and want or need to update your skills, retrain or gain an official qualification in the job you are doing? If any of these questions describe your situation, this section will help you to think about how you can return to work, improve your education level or find a new job.

This section is very different from the rest of the book because when it comes to personal development, there are no hard regulations about what is right and wrong. The aim is to give you different options so that you can find the solution that is right for you. Although there is guidance on the rules, bear in mind that there will always be exceptions to the rule.

Many parents who have not worked for a while believe that the only **skills** they have are concerned with bringing up children and they often lack **confidence** that those skills can be used in the workplace. Helping you to think about what skills you have to offer an employer is an important first step towards getting a job. Although you may not have recent work experience, you have some positive attributes to offer. Once you have worked out what these are, you need to think about the **next steps** to take in order to get the job you want.

If you feel that you want to **return to learning and gain qualifications**, you have to consider what level of skills you have and at what level you want to train or retrain. There are organisations that can help you. If you decide that education or training is the right path for you, you also need to investigate what **financial support** is available to help you do this.

Alternatively, you may be eligible to take part in one of the Government's **New Deal** initiatives.

CONFIDENCE-BUILDING

If you have not worked for a while, you may feel that you don't have any skills to offer an employer. This chapter will help you identify what skills you may have developed during your time at home that you can apply at work.

20

20 CONFIDENCE-BUILDING

"I have been looking after children for so long that I don't know what else I can do."

"I don't want to return to the job I did before, I want something closer to home."

"I haven't worked out of the home for so long my work skills are out of date."

Sound familiar?

Have you not done any paid work for a while? Do you feel that you have lost confidence in your ability to go out to work? Many parents who have been out of paid work but have been bringing up their children lack the confidence they need to get back into paid work. This chapter is designed to help you establish what skills you do have and how you might apply them to a job.

I have not done any paid work for a while, what do I have to offer an employer?

To help you think about what you have to offer an employer, consider all of the following:

- your experience
- your skills
- your personal qualities

YOUR EXPERIENCE

From every experience in life we learn different lessons about attitudes and behaviour. You might have experienced one or more of the following:

- moving house
- marriage/divorce
- caring for children or an elderly person
- death of a family member, friend or relative
- falling into debt
- travel
- living alone
- personal achievement
- voluntary activities, fun runs or fundraising

Exercise

Think about the experiences that you have had and the impact those experiences have had on your character. Ask yourself:

- were you stronger than you thought?
- were you able to cope under pressure?
- did you try something for the first time and handle it well?
- did you set yourself a goal that you believed to be unachievable, and reach it
    - such as losing weight or running in a local charity race?

YOUR SKILLS

Everyday life teaches us skills through our hobbies, relationships, travel and daily routines.

Exercise

Consider the skills that you have developed through the activities you have done in your daily life. To help you, below is a list of some of the key skills that are used in the workplace – you will be better at some than you are at others:

- communication – written and oral skills
- computer skills
- counselling

- financial planning/numeracy skills
- leadership
- manual or technical skills
- negotiation
- people skills
- planning and organisation
- problem-solving
- teaching
- teamwork
- time management

All of the skills listed above are useful at work and if you have not been working for a while, you may *think* that you lack many of these skills. However, the role of a parent, for example, uses many of the same skills as an office manager, such as multi-tasking, time-management and organisational skills.

The checklists below give more detail about some of the skills listing some activities that you may have done which demonstrate the skills that you have developed. This exercise may help you to think a little more confidently about what you have to offer.

Communicating skills	Planning and Organising
☐ Being a good listener	☐ Organising others
☐ Speaking clearly	☐ Making arrangements
☐ Writing letters	☐ Working to deadlines
☐ Starting a conversation	☐ Working without close supervision
☐ Speaking clearly on the phone	☐ Handling a variety of tasks
☐ Asking for help	☐ Dealing well with a crisis
☐ Stating own opinions	☐ Taking difficult decisions
☐ Giving instructions	☐ Finding new ways of doing things
☐ Solving arguments	☐ Financial planning for a household
☐ Negotiating	☐ Managing time
☐ Explaining	☐ Adapting to changing circumstances

People skills	Manual Skills
☐ Dealing with different types of people	☐ Manual skills
☐ Persuading people	☐ Driving a car
☐ Showing patience	☐ Cooking
☐ Being approachable	☐ Making or mending clothes
☐ Understanding how others feel	☐ Changing a plug
☐ Advising	☐ Painting and decorating
☐ Counselling	☐ Following instructions in a manual
☐ Assertiveness	☐ Applying first aid
☐ Taking criticism well	☐ Typing
	☐ Using a computer

Exercise

Write a list of the skills you have to offer. Next to each one, write at least one example or activity that you do (or have done) as evidence of this.

For example, in Planning and Organisation:

- I am the one who organises the activities for my friends or my child
- I often juggle many tasks at one time

You may therefore be able to tick "organising others", "making arrangements", "handling a variety of tasks" and some others. These are useful skills to have at work.

YOUR PERSONAL QUALITIES

Personal characteristics are just as important as skills and experiences. Your employer may be able to provide you with training to teach you how to do the job, therefore the type of person you are may be more significant if you are to fit in with other employees.

How would you describe yourself?

Exercise

Think of 5 words that sum up your qualities. Below is a list of some that you might consider apply to you:

Adaptable	Cheerful
Confident	Conscientious
Creative	Determined
Diplomatic	Energetic
Enthusiastic	Flexible
Friendly	Honest
Humorous	Imaginative
Independent	Innovative
Logical	Loyal
Mature	Modest
Motivated	Open-minded
Optimistic	Organised
Patient	Practical
Precise	Quick learner
Reliable	Sensible
Sensitive	Thoughtful
Tidy	Tolerant
Trustworthy	Use your initiative

SUMMARY

Now that you have a list of the skills and personal qualities that you have to offer an employer, you can start to think about what work you might want to do. Chapter 21 will help you consider the next steps you need to take.

Visit the Women Returner's Network website for an interactive version of this chapter and more exercises to help you: www.women-returners.co.uk or call their helpline on 01245 263 796.

TAKING THE FIRST STEPS

Once you know what skills and qualities you have to offer an employer, this chapter can help you to work out the best way to get the job that you want.

21

21 TAKING THE FIRST STEPS

After reading the previous chapter you will have identified some of the skills and qualities you have to offer an employer. However, you may still be unsure about the best way to get the job that you want.

If you are thinking of choosing a career that you have not previously worked in, you have 2 questions to consider:

1. How can I get some experience?

2. What could I learn to make myself more marketable to employers?

To give an example, Kelly used to work in an office and does not want to go back to doing that. Her passion is gardening, but she has never worked in this business before. Overleaf is a mindmap of the different paths that Kelly could take to help her begin a career in gardening.

Exercise

Think about what it is that you would like to do, and draw yourself a mindmap like the one overleaf with your possible options.

If you are still unsure about what you can do, here are some suggested sources to help you:

- **reference books**   your local library has books describing occupations and directories with thousands of jobs and information on necessary training, qualifications and salary
- **job adverts** – buy your local paper when they have the largest recruitment section and study the advertisements and compare the qualifications, skills and personal qualities that employers are looking for with those on your list
- **professional journals** – read articles that will inform you about current issues the profession is concerned with
- **friends, relations and neighbours** – ask them what they do,

KELLY'S MINDMAP

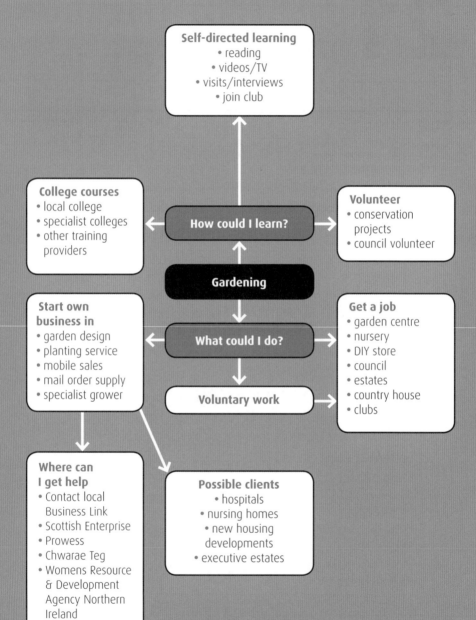

Self-directed learning
- reading
- videos/TV
- visits/interviews
- join club

College courses
- local college
- specialist colleges
- other training providers

How could I learn?

Volunteer
- conservation projects
- council volunteer

Gardening

Start own business in
- garden design
- planting service
- mobile sales
- mail order supply
- specialist grower

What could I do?

Get a job
- garden centre
- nursery
- DIY store
- council
- estates
- country house
- clubs

Voluntary work

Where can I get help
- Contact local Business Link
- Scottish Enterprise
- Prowess
- Chwarae Teg
- Womens Resource & Development Agency Northern Ireland

Possible clients
- hospitals
- nursing homes
- new housing developments
- executive estates

what they enjoy or don't enjoy, how they got their job and what qualifications are needed
- **work experience** – you could approach an employer to see if it would be possible for you to spend a few days in a department that interests you, thereby gaining valuable experience and contacts. There is usually no pay but sometimes they will pay your travel costs
- **temporary work** – doing temporary work in different organisations and departments is a good way to gain an insight into the work involved in a wide range of occupations
- **internet** – the internet is available free in many places – try your local library. It would be good computer practice too, and you can look for jobs, get background information on companies and research other possible areas of work

Kelly's mindmap was created by the Women Returner's Network (WRN). This organisation can help women think about what options are available to them when returning to work. They can be contacted through their website at www.women-returners.co.uk

YOUR ACTION PLAN

Once you have worked out what you need to do, you may want to write an action plan to help you achieve your goals:

1. set yourself some goals – both short-term and long-term

2. think about how you can achieve the goals you have set

3. identify the people who can help and support you

4. set yourself deadlines for achieving some of these steps

The WRN website (see above) can also help you to write your own personal action plan.

EVALUATING A JOB

If you do not want to return to the job that you were doing before you had children, but are not sure what you want to do, you will need to research other jobs. When looking at potential jobs, think about the following questions to help you work out if it is going to be the right job for you:

- what hours does the job require?
- what particular skills are required?
- how far away from home is the job?
- how long will it take you to get to work?
- does the job require any physical ability that may cause problems for you?
- what qualifications and experience do you have that will be applicable?

LEARNING AND QUALIFICATIONS

There are a number of training routes and advisory services, all of which can help you get back into the workplace. This chapter identifies some of the education and training options available and helps you decide what kind of assistance you might need.

22

22 LEARNING AND QUALIFICATIONS

Once you have an idea of what skills you have and what type of job you want to do, if you want to gain a qualification to enable you to get a particular job or to get a promotion at work, this chapter will help you identify what type of qualification might be right for you.

WHAT LEVEL OF SKILL DO YOU HAVE ALREADY?

How would you describe your level of qualifications? Do you have basic skills needs, or are you in the low-, medium-, or high-level skill group? The table below helps you identify your level.

What are my qualifications and skill levels?

Skill Level	Qualifications		
Basic Skills	I have difficulty with reading, writing and numbers and I often find it hard to help my child with homework		
Low-level Skills	I have no GCSEs, GNVQs or O levels at grades A* to C	AND	I don't have an NVQ
	I have less than 5 GCSEs, GNVQs or O levels at grades A* to C	OR	I have an NVQ Level 1
Medium-level Skills	I have 5 or more GCSEs GNVQs or O levels at grades A to C **OR** I have a BTEC National Diploma	OR	I have an NVQ Level 2 **OR** I have an Apprenticeship
High-level Skills	I have one or more A-levels **OR** I have a BTEC Higher National Diploma	OR	I have an NVQ Level 3 **OR** I have an Advanced Apprenticeship
	I have a degree	OR	I have an NVQ Level 4 **OR** I have a Foundation degree
	I have a Masters degree (MA)	OR	I have an NVQ Level 5
	I have a PhD	OR	I have an NVQ Level 6

What are Basic Skills?

Basic Skills is the new name for what used to be called the 3Rs – reading, writing and arithmetic. There is no rule to say what standard of Basic Skills adults are expected to reach, but a good guide would be that you should aim to reach the same standard expected of 16-year-olds – good enough to get at least C grades in GCSE English and Mathematics.

As many as 26 million adults in the UK may not have reached this standard – so if you have Basic Skills needs remember that you are not alone.

Basic Skills programmes to help you gain these skills are available in a wide variety of places, including:

- in Further and Adult Education Colleges
- in the workplace
- at your local Jobcentre Plus
- in prisons
- in community centres
- in family literacy centres at primary schools

There are new short courses to get you up to the standard quickly.

What should I do if I have low-level skills?

Many adults have poor grades from school or no qualifications related to their work. The good news is you don't have to go back to school to re-sit your GCSEs. It would be more useful for you to get yourself some qualifications related to your work, in fact, something that will give you the skills to get the kind of job you have always wanted.

What is the National Qualifications Framework?

Before you start thinking about getting some work-related qualifications it helps to know a little bit about the National Qualifications Framework. This organises qualifications into levels depending on how advanced the qualifications are and what grade of worker they are intended for.

A guide to levels of qualification and their associated job grades

Level 1: Assistant

Level 2: Skilled worker

Level 3: Supervisor, technician, or craftsperson

Level 4: Manager or specialist technical worker

Level 5: Senior manager, chartered or professional worker

The table above provides a rough idea of what qualification goes with which job grade. Those qualified to **Level 1** might work as assistants. They have the knowledge and skill to perform useful work but rely on more qualified staff to make decisions, sort out problems and arrange their working day.

Someone qualified to **Level 2** is a more independent worker. They have enough skill and knowledge to make decisions on what to do in given situations, can diagnose and sort out their own problems and prioritise their working day. To give an example, a plumber who can call at your home, figure out what's wrong, decide what to do and fix the problem without having to be told how by someone else would be a good example of someone qualified to Level 2.

People with qualifications to **Level 3** usually work in a supervisory position, or in positions where they are expected to have either a much wider knowledge or specialist knowledge of the most advanced or complicated aspects.

An example is skilled technical staff and craftspeople who are often qualified to Level 3, such as accountants.

A manager within a company would probably have a **Level 4** qualification such as a degree and they would be responsible for a department perhaps, with skilled workers at Levels 3, 2 and 1 working for them. Graduates with degrees are often taken on by companies and trained to go straight in at managerial level.

Those with **Level 5** qualifications might be senior managers in an organisation or be Chartered or Professional Workers who have passed an examination to become a member of a professional body or chartered institute – a body that sets the highest standards of qualification within a profession.

DO I NEED TO IMPROVE MY SKILLS?

The skill level you need depends on the type of job you want to do. The Medium-level Skills indicated on page 210 is fast becoming the minimum standard expected of workers. Those who do not have 5 GCSEs, O-levels or a National Vocational Qualification (NVQ) above Level 1 should think about updating and improving their qualifications.

Learning for free

You might be able to get free courses to help you improve your reading, writing and number skills.

If you claim a benefit or rely on somebody else who claims a benefit, you may get your fees for courses paid in full or in part.

Entitlement to Level 2 and Level 3 qualifications

If you are aged over 19 years, you are entitled to study for a Level 2 (or equivalent) qualification without having to pay course fees.

If you are aged 19–25 and doing your first Level 3 (or equivalent) qualification, you do not have to pay fees for your course.

Free learning online

Anyone can learn on the Internet for free:

- Learndirect offers free taster courses in literacy, numeracy and computer skills (see page 226)
- the BBC offers free courses in literacy and numeracy, computers and the internet, languages and many more subjects

You can get free Internet access at UK online centres and libraries. For information about your nearest UK online centre, call the Learndirect helpline 0800 100 900 or visit the website at: www.dfes.gov.uk/get-on

NATIONAL VOCATIONAL QUALIFICATION (NVQ)

NVQs are the main qualifications to consider if you want to get qualified in your chosen area of work. There are over 250 different kinds of NVQ and there is one to suit you, whether you are or want to be a butcher (NVQ in Meat and Poultry Processing), a baker (NVQ in Bakery) or even a candlestick maker (NVQ in Performing Manufacturing Operations).

What are NVQs?

NVQs are a way of gaining a qualification "on the job", they are a "hands on" qualification. You receive training from your employer while you are at work. When you are ready, and feel you have reached the required standard, you are assessed.

The idea of an NVQ is to see if you can cope with the unplanned and unexpected, respond to additional demands, requests, pressures and problems that arise in jobs all the time and every day.

How are they assessed?

- there are no formal exams, you are assessed in the workplace completing normal work activities
- during assessment they are looking for your ability to apply all your knowledge and skills in the workplace to get jobs done on time and to the required standard

Who can take NVQ courses?

- NVQs are open to everyone at any age or stage of their career
- you can start at whatever level suits you
- there are no formal entry requirements, although the higher levels need more experience
- you can either get on to an NVQ through your employer or by contacting Learndirect (see page 250)

Do I have to go to college?

You can either study full-time at college, or you can do it at the same time as working if you are already working. NVQs will require a work placement in order for key competencies to be assessed and qualifications completed.

If you decide to study full-time, you need to find a work placement to undertake some of the assessment, this can be a voluntary or temporary placement. Further Education Colleges and training providers can help you organise your work placements.

Where can I find out more?
- if you are already in work, your employer, human resources or personnel department will be able to let you know if any programmes are available
- your trade union representative will also have helpful information
- it is always a good idea to talk to people who are doing, or have completed, NVQs themselves
- Local Further Education Colleges have information on all the NVQ programmes they offer
- you can also contact your local Jobcentre Plus
- the Qualifications and Curriculum Authority (QCA) will also provide information. See the website www.qca.org.uk or call their enquiry line on 020 7509 5556
- call Learndirect (see page 250)

AN APPRENTICESHIP

What is it?
An apprenticeship allows you to get on-the-job training, study for a nationally recognised qualification such as an NVQ, and get paid at the same time. Apprenticeships are designed to meet the needs of a particular industry. There are over 150 different apprenticeship programmes covering over 80 industries including engineering, retail, information technology, floristry, accounting, construction and financial services. This provides a great variety of occupations in which to work and train.

Who can do an apprenticeship?
- apprenticeships are available for young people between the ages of 16 and 24 years
- you are normally required to have at least 5 GCSEs at grades A to C but entry requirements are flexible because Apprenticeships are not just based on academic achievement

- practical skills count, and an interest in the work – employers value those who are keen to learn

Where can I find out more?

There are several ways to become an apprentice. You can apply for an apprenticeship online at www.apprenticeships.org.uk/youngpeople/whatnext or through the Connexions Service, see page 228.

THE OPEN UNIVERSITY

The Open University (OU) is the UK's only university dedicated to distance learning. This means that you can learn in your own time by studying at home and sometimes attending classes in your locality. Contact with your tutor is otherwise by telephone or email when required. Most universities offer distance-learning courses.

For many courses there is no requirement for you to have previous qualifications. You have to be aged 18 when you start the course, but there is no upper age limit.

Nearly all students at the OU are studying part-time.

For all general and course-related enquiries:

Student Registration and Enquiry Service, The Open University, PO Box 197, Milton Keynes, MK7 6BJ. Telephone 0870 333 4340

Email: general-enquiries@open.ac.uk or visit the OU website at www3.open.ac.uk/courses for course information or www3.open.ac.uk/about for general information.

FURTHER INFORMATION

This chapter has provided guidance on which training and qualifications are available if you want to train, retrain or gain qualifications. There are many organisations that can help you get more information and apply for courses, see page 225.

FINANCIAL SUPPORT FOR LEARNING

If you are returning to education or entering training there may be some financial support that can help you with the associated costs. This chapter outlines what financial support is available.

23

23 FINANCIAL SUPPORT FOR LEARNING

As described in chapter 22 (see page 213), all adults, whether in work or unemployed, are entitled to participate in training and achieve a qualification up to NVQ Level 2 without being charged tuition fees. If you are between 19 and 25 years old, you are entitled to study for a qualification up to Level 3 without being charged tuition fees.

Also, most courses that are available through Further Education Colleges are free of tuition fees to all unemployed people.

In addition, there is a range of financial support available to help you participate in training and education.

HELP WITH THE COSTS OF LEARNING

The Learning and Skills Council (LSC) operates a range of programmes to help students with the costs associated with their Further Education courses. These programmes are intended to assist those students who may otherwise have difficulties in completing their course because of financial considerations.

These programmes are:

- Adult Learning Grant
- Career Development Loans
- Learner Support Fund
- Dance and Drama Award
- Childcare Support
- Education Maintenance Allowance

You may be able to apply for support from more than one programme or fund but this will depend on your eligibility, and the rules of each scheme. You cannot, for example, receive a Dance and Drama Award *and* an Education Maintenance Allowance.

ADULT LEARNING GRANT

What is it?

The Adult Learning Grant (ALG) is a sum of money offered to adults on a low income who wish to take up full-time learning. The ALG is aimed at adults studying for their first full qualification at Level 2 or Level 3.

If you are eligible, the ALG will pay you up to £30 a week – depending on your income – during your term time. This grant will be paid directly into your bank account each week.

Who can claim it?

You can claim the ALG if you live in England, are aged over 19 and studying full-time for your first full Level 2 or Level 3 qualification.

People receiving benefits because they are unemployed are not eligible for the grant. Jobcentre Plus can let you know about your entitlements and where you can get advice on learning.

For further information call Learndirect on 0800 100 900 or visit www.lifelonglearning.dfes.gov.uk/adultlearninggrant

CAREER DEVELOPMENT LOANS

What are these?

Career Development Loans (CDLs) are commercial loans to help pay for the cost of vocational learning or education. You do not make any repayments on the loan while you are in learning, but when your education has finished, you then repay the loan to the bank over an agreed period (usually up to 2 years) at a fixed rate of interest. CDLs are currently available through Barclays, the Co-Operative Bank and the Royal Bank of Scotland.

How much can I receive?

You can apply to borrow anything between £300 and £8,000 to fund up to 2 years' learning plus up to 1 year's practical work experience where it forms part of the course.

Who can apply?

Anyone aged 18 or over can apply for a CDL but you must be a resident in Great Britain and the course must be vocational, that is, work-related.

Full details of the programme, its eligibility criteria and application forms, are available from the CDL information line on 0800 585 5005 or visit the website at www.direct.gov.uk/EducationAndLearning/AdultLearning/CareerDevelopmentLoans

THE LEARNER SUPPORT FUND

What is this?

The Learner Support Fund (LSF) helps students on part-time or full-time FE courses who need additional help with some of the costs associated with learning, such as course equipment, childcare, or some of the costs of accommodation if it is necessary to study away from home.

Who can apply?

Hardship funds are available to cover immediate basic needs. You can apply for hardship funds even if you are receiving other forms of learner support, such as the Educational Maintenance Allowance or the ALG. Your college will assess your application, and you may be asked to provide evidence, such as a bank statement, that you have no other funds to cover your needs. If you think you might need to apply, you should contact your college's Student Support office for more information. If you are studying at a School Sixth Form, you should contact your year tutor or the student awards officer.

You can apply for a **Residential Bursary** if you are on a full-time FE course that lasts for 10 weeks or more in one academic year and if the college is too far from home for daily travel. The Residential Bursary supports learners who are:

- attending one of the 51 specialist colleges of agriculture and horticulture, or art and design; you can get a list of these colleges by logging on to www.dfes.gov.uk/financialhelp
- the bursary helps with the costs of accommodation and may help with travel costs; if you wish to apply for a bursary you should speak to the student support officer at the college

If you are not intending to study at one of these colleges and the course you want to study is not available within reasonable daily travelling distance, you may be entitled to support from the **FE Residential Support Programme**. Support from this programme is income-assessed, and is only available to learners aged over 16 who are studying full-time for a Level 2 or Level 3, LSC-funded course. It will provide you with help with the costs of accommodation and may be able to help with some travel costs. For further information or an application pack, phone the helpline on 0161 234 7021 or email residential.edpilot@manchester.gov.uk

DANCE AND DRAMA AWARD

What is this?

Funds are available to help individuals who want to become professional dancers, actors or stage managers. Dance and Drama Awards (DaDAs) can offer reduced tuition fees and help with living and learning costs based on your household income. They are only available at schools/colleges participating in the scheme, and only if you take one of the specified courses.

How can I apply?

You need to apply directly to the participating dance and drama schools/ colleges and audition for a place. The school will then select those with the most potential to succeed in the profession and can award a DaDA.

Information about which schools are eligible to offer Awards and how to apply can be found by calling 0845 602 2260 to order booklet D6, or by going online at www.direct.gov.uk/danceanddrama or you can email dada@lsc.gov.uk.

CHILDCARE SUPPORT
CARE TO LEARN

What is it?

Care to Learn (C2L) provides financial assistance with the costs of childcare for young parents who want to continue in education or training. This can include the time you are at college, in a work placement or doing course work, as well as additional costs that you incur travelling between your childcare provider and your learning provider. The course you choose doesn't have to lead to a qualification.

Who can apply?

In order to be eligible for C2L support, you must live in England, you must use registered childcare (see page 85) , and your learning must be publicly funded. You must be the main carer for your child – fathers are eligible if they are the main carer – and you must be under the age of 20 on the day you start your course.

How much is it?

If you are eligible, your childcare costs (including any additional travel costs) are paid up to a maximum of £155 a week, or £170 if you live in London. These rates are available from 1 August 2006.

For more information, you can call the Care to Learn helpline on 0845 600 2809 or visit www.dfes.gov.uk/caretolearn

Other financial help with childcare

If you need help with childcare costs and are over 20 when your learning starts, you should contact the **Student Support office** at your college to discuss an application for LSF (see page 220).

If you are in a Sixth-Form College or a School Sixth Form, you may be eligible for support from the **20+ Childcare in Sixth-Form Colleges and School Sixth Forms Fund**. Applications to this Fund are assessed against your household income. If you live at home, this will be your parents' income. You can apply if you are studying full-time or part-time, but the amount of help that you get will be based on the amount of time that you are actually studying or attending the college. If you would like to apply to this Fund, you can get an application form by phoning 0161 234 7026.

Details of the help available from your Local Authority and how to apply for it are given in a guide *Childcare grant and other support for student parents in higher education in 2006/2007.*

There is also a factsheet called *Applying for the Childcare Grant in 2006/2007 – What you need to know (S/ACCG/V5)*. You can get a copy of the guide and factsheet from your Local Authority, or copies of the guide can be ordered from 0800 731 9133 or by visiting the online website at www.studentsupportdirect.co.uk

EDUCATION MAINTENANCE ALLOWANCE (EMA)

What is it?

The Education Maintenance Allowance (EMA) is a weekly payment of up to £30, which is paid directly to young people (aged 16–19) who continue in Further Education after the end of their compulsory schooling. This fund is only available in England.

The weekly payment is intended to help with the day-to-day costs while you attend college or training. You can use it for travel, books and equipment, for example.

The payments are paid directly into your bank account, during term-time only. You can get bonuses of £100 depending on the progress you make with your course. If you return for a second year, that can amount to £500 potential extra money over the 2 years.

Who can claim it?

You can claim EMA if:

- your 16th birthday is between 1 September 2006 and 31 August 2007
- your household income is less than £30,810 per year (If you are living with your parents, you will need to check with them about this)
- you meet the residency rules outlined on the application form

- you are studying, or have applied to study, for at least 12 hours in the Sixth Form, at a Further Education College or at a training provider. This means up to and including level 3, for example AS/A level, GCSEs, GNVQs, NVQs and other courses
- you are doing a course that leads to an apprenticeship

How much is it?

It is a weekly payment of £10, £20 or £30 depending on your household income. To work out how much, see below. If, for example, your household income is:

Household income for academic year 2006–7	Weekly payment
Up to £20,817	£30
£20,818 to £25,521	£20
£25,522 to £30,810	£10

For further information and to request an application form, visit the website https://students.emasys1.dfes.gov.uk or call the EMA Helpline 0808 1016219.

FURTHER INFORMATION

- If you would like further information on the range of financial support that is available, it can be found at www.dfes.gov.uk/financialhelp

- The Directgov website www.direct.gov.uk also contains information on learner support

- If you want more information about any other funds, visit www.support4learning.org.uk or contact your Local Authority. You can get the contact details of your Local Authority by calling DfES on 0870 0002288

ORGANISATIONS TO HELP YOU RETURN TO EDUCATION

There are many organisations that can help you return to education or training. This chapter outlines the main ones.

24

24 ORGANISATIONS TO HELP YOU RETURN TO EDUCATION

Taking the first steps back to training and employment can be a daunting and confusing task but it is easier if you know where to begin to find the right information, advice and guidance. Listed below are some of the national organisations that are able to help guide you on your path.

THE LEARNDIRECT SERVICE

The Learndirect Service provides a telephone helpline and website where adults can get information, advice and guidance on their learning needs. The service is free, confidential, and impartial, and is delivered by qualified advisers.

You can call the telephone helpline free on 0800 100 900, 7 days a week, 8am–10pm. You can also visit the website on www.learndirect.co.uk

Learndirect Advice Service can tell you about computer-based courses in your local area, as well as any daytime or evening courses that are available at your local college, library, community or day-care centre. They can also refer you to local advisory services that can offer face-to-face advice.

The helpline provides information on courses and learning opportunities and in-depth careers advice. It also offers information on careers, returning to work, funding and childcare. The helpline advice is impartial and therefore refers callers to both Learndirect services and also other courses and training services. The helpline is available in English and Welsh, Punjabi, Bengali/Sylheti, Somali, Gujarati, Urdu, Polish, French and Farsi.

NEXTSTEP PROVIDERS

Nextstep offers information advice and guidance to adults aged 20 and over in England. Nextstep aims to:

- help you link your personal interests and skills to your own job or career needs
- identify the skills you may require and refer you to other sources of help if you need to improve your reading, writing and maths
- give you advice about the financial support available
- give you basic advice about the services available after being made redundant, including how to access them and where to go
- give you advice on ways to search and apply for jobs, such as writing a CV and interview skills

You can find out more information, or locate your nearest Nextstep office on their website at www.nextstep.org.uk

CAREERS WALES

In Wales, careers guidance is offered to all age groups through the Careers Wales service. It directs you to the relevant Learndirect courses but also has 12 careers centres and a website dedicated to information advice and guidance.

For more information, visit their website: www.careerswales.com

CAREERS SCOTLAND

Careers Scotland has website and helpline which provides information, advice and guidance on careers and employment for everyone in Scotland. For more information, call them on 08457 8 502 502 or visit their website at www.careers-scotland.org.uk

NORTHERN IRELAND

A similar service of career and employment advice to that in England is available by contacting the Department of Employment and Learning in Northern Ireland. You can call them on 0209 025 7538 or visit the website at www.delni.gov.uk

JOBCENTRE PLUS

There is a wide range of training and employment services available through Jobcentre Plus, which is the employment and benefit service. However, your local Jobcentre Plus can assist you even if you are not currently in receipt of work-related benefits, although the options that may be available could depend on your current circumstances.

Jobcentre Plus provides an online job search facility at www.jobcentreplus.gov.uk/JCP/Customers/

If you are not sure where your nearest Jobcentre Plus office is located, you can also find this through the website at www.jobcentreplus.gov.uk or ring 0845 6060 with your queries.

CONNEXIONS

If you are aged between 16 and 19, or up to 25, have a disability or learning difficulty, and are wanting to get a job, then Connexions is the main service to advise with your learning and work needs. They can also give advice on careers, childcare, benefits and relationships. There are Connexions centres in most towns and you can find their details in your local phone book. Or you can visit their website at www.connexions-direct.com and click on "local services"

You can call Connexions Direct on 080 800 13219.

When you make contact with Connexions, the personal adviser will need some basic information so that they can help you. This basic information consists of your contact details and information about how you have progressed through learning in the past.

An adviser will then work on a personal development plan that is best for you. This could include you being referred to training and employment through established programmes or to a course at your local college, or with a local training provider. Your adviser can even arrange for you to learn from home if this is an arrangement you would prefer.

ACCESS TO FURTHER AND HIGHER EDUCATION

- Further Education (FE) refers to education after the age of 16 and it includes a wide range of activity from basic to high skill levels but most Further Education is for intermediate skills and vocational training routes
- Higher Education (HE) means graduate and post-graduate education and the typical route into Higher Education requires academic qualifications (usually 3 A-levels at grades A–C); however, there are a number of other entry routes available to mature students who have been out of the education system for some time

FE colleges offer specific Access Programmes to enable older students to enter Higher Education. The main aim of Access programmes is to prepare adult learners for degree-level education and a significant number of students enter Higher Education from Access programmes.

The University and Colleges Admissions Service (UCAS) has developed a new website dedicated to Access issues. This provides a way in which you are able to enter university without having to sit A-levels. Visit their website at www.ucas.com/access or call them for information on 0870 1122211. Their telephone line is open Monday to Friday from 8.30am to 6pm.

Successful completion of some vocational courses (at NVQ Level 3 and above) can also lead to degree-level courses; for example, if you have taken and passed a Heathcare NVQ, you could study Nursing.

NEW DEALS

The government has programmes to help those who have been unemployed for some time get back into work. This chapter outlines the New Deal schemes that may be available and are applicable to your circumstances.

25

25 NEW DEALS

What are they?

New Deals are government-supported programmes that have been designed to help with problems of long-term unemployment. Their aim is to improve people's chances of finding and keeping a job.

You will receive the support of a New Deal Personal Adviser who is committed to helping you tackle any barriers you may face in getting into work, finding a job, or getting training or work experience to help you move towards getting a job or becoming self-employed.

New Deal for Young People and New Deal 25+

- New Deal for Young People gives anyone under the age of 25 the opportunity to explore the different work options available
- New Deal 25+ gives people over the age of 25 a chance to review their situation, take the skills and experience they have already and build on them to create better opportunities for work

Who can join?

New Deal for Young People and New Deal 25+ are compulsory if:

- **New Deal for Young People** you are aged between 18 and 24 years and have been claiming Jobseeker's Allowance (JSA) continuously for 6 months or more
- **New Deal for 25+** you are aged 25 years or more and have been claiming JSA continuously for 18 months or more, or have been unemployed for 18 out of the last 21 months

If you cannot apply because you do not fit into either of the above categories, you could get entry into a compulsory New Deal Programme if you are a member of a disadvantaged group such as lone parent or disabled.

How to begin

After speaking to your local Jobcentre Plus office, you will be invited to meet with your New Deal Personal Adviser who will be your contact throughout the New Deal programme. It is their job to:

- get to know a little about you so you end up with a job you enjoy
- discuss with you what kind of job you would like to get
- draw up an action plan to help you get that job
- help you look for and apply for suitable jobs
- help you overcome anything that might be stopping you getting work – this could include reasons such as having a problem with reading and writing and difficulties with travelling to childcare or to a workplace
- identify any extra help you might need, such as writing letters of application or the techniques of job searching

All of this takes place during the first stage of New Deal known as the **Gateway**, which lasts for up to 4 months, and consists of a number of informal discussions.

If you haven't got a job during the Gateway stage, your New Deal Personal Adviser then arranges a package of full-time help to meet your specific needs. This second stage of New Deal is known as:

New Deal for Young People – **Option**

New Deal for 25+ – **Intensive Activity Period**

During this stage you receive a training allowance equivalent to your Jobseeker's Allowance and you may also receive a top-up payment of £15.38 per week. Depending on what is best for you, this stage might include:

- work experience/work placements with an employer or voluntary organisation
- training for a specific job
- courses to develop the skills that employers want
- practical help with applying for jobs
- interview practice

If, at the end of the Option or Intensive Activity Period you haven't managed to secure a job, you will return to the Jobcentre Plus to make a new claim for Jobseeker's Allowance. This is the final stage, known as **Follow-through**. During this stage, your New Deal Personal Adviser will continue to help you search for and secure a job.

NEW DEAL FOR LONE PARENTS

What is New Deal for Lone Parents?

New Deal for Lone Parents (NDLP) is a voluntary programme with a package of support specifically designed to help lone parents get work.

Who can join New Deal for Lone Parents?

You can join NDLP if:

- your youngest child under 16 years old
- you are not working, or working less than 16 hours a week

How do I begin?

You work with one person, called a personal adviser, who talks through your situation, gives advice and helps you to find whatever support you need.

Your personal adviser can offer practical help and advice:

- if you are not sure what you want to do
- when you need advice on your options and planning ahead
- when you are looking for work
- when you want to get training for a job
- after you start work

As well as this your personal adviser can:

- calculate how much better off you could be in a job
- explain the effect that starting work may have on your existing benefits or Tax Credits
- explain what benefits or Tax Credits you may be entitled to when you get into work

- get you specialist employment advice if you have a disability or health problem
- help you identify good quality registered childcare in your area
- help you with expenses to attend any meetings, job interviews or training they arrange for you, including fares and registered childcare costs

If you want to find out more about New Deal for Lone Parents or you would like to arrange to see a personal adviser, call their freephone information line on 0800 868 868.

FURTHER INFORMATION

- If you have any questions about New Deal, call the New Deal helpline on 0845 606 2626. They are open 7am–11pm, 7 days a week or visit the website at www.jobcentreplus.gov.uk

USEFUL ORGANISATIONS

4 Children

5 Greenwich View Place, London E14 9NN
Tel: 020 7512 2112
Fax: 020 753760121
Email: info@children.org.uk
Website: www.4children.org.uk

4 Children works to ensure that children's needs are met in the community through providing information and guidance, influencing national policy, and developing programmes to tackle issues such as social exclusion.

4 Nations Child Policy Network

Email: info@childpolicy.org.uk
Website: www.childpolicy.org.uk

The 4 Nations Child Policy Network is a partnership between the National Children's Bureau (with NCVCCO), Children in Northern Ireland, Children in Scotland and Children in Wales. The Network provides bulletins with information on the latest news concerning child policy matters.

ACAS (Advisory, Conciliation and Arbitration Service)

Brandon House, 180 Borough High Street, London SE1 1LW
Tel: 020 7210 3613
Helpline: 08457 474747
Website: www.acas.org.uk

ACAS aims to improve organisations and working life through better employment relations by providing up-to-date information, independent advice, and training for employers and employees.

Accor Services UK

50 Vauxhall Road, London SW1V 2RS
Tel: 0845 3304411
Email: ccv@accorservices.co.uk
Website: www.accorservices.co.uk

Accor Services is a provider of human resources services, including Childcare Voucher schemes for employers.

Action for Blind People

14–16 Verney Road, London SE16 3DZ
Tel: 020 7635 4800
Fax: 020 7635 4900
Helpline: 0800 915 4666
Email: info@afbp.org
Website: www.afbp.org

Action for Blind People provides practical support for blind and partially sighted people through work, housing, leisure and support.

Advisory Centre for Education (ACE)

1c Aberdeen Studios, 22 Highbury Grove, London N5 2DQ
Tel: 020 7704 3370
Fax: 020 7354 9069
Advice line: 0808 800 5793
Exclusion information line: 020 7704 9822
Website: www.ace-ed.org.uk
ACE is an independent advice centre for parents, offering information on many topics concerned with state education in England and Wales for children aged 5–16 years, such as exclusion from school, bullying and special educational needs.

Association for Women in Science and Engineering (AwiSE)

59 Portland Place, London W1B 1QW
Tel: 020 7060 4571
Fax: 020 7060 1571
Email: info@awise.org
Website: www.awise.org

AWiSE is a multi-disciplinary membership organisation composed of individuals, businesses, associations, institutions and other organisations, which aims to advance the interests of women in science, engineering and technology (SET).

BBC Parenting

Website: www.bbc.co.uk/parenting

The BBC Parenting website is a one-stop shop for advice about bringing up your children and your role as parents.

British Au Pair Agencies Association (BAPAA)

Trafalgar House, Grenville Place, London NW7 3SA
Website: www.bapaa.org.uk

BAPAA is a non-commercial association of agencies within the UK that works to ensure that a high standard of service is delivered to families and au pairs.

Business Link

Tel: 0845 600 9006
Website: www.businesslink.org

The website provides a wide range of helpful information for small businesses, and the contact details of local Business Link services. Small businesses can register to receive reminders and updates about changes to employment law.

Care Standards Inspectorate for Wales (CSIW)

National Assembly for Wales, Cardiff Bay, Cardiff CF99 1NA
Tel: 029 20 825111
Website: www.csiw.wales.gov.uk

CSIW regulates social care, Early Years and private and voluntary health care services in Wales in accordance with regulations and national minimum standards.

Care Standards Tribunal (CST)

Care Standards Tribunal, 18 Pocock Street, London SE1 0BW
Tel: 020 7960 0660
Fax: 020 7960 0661
Email: CST@CST.gsi.gov.uk
Website: www.carestandardstribunal.gov.uk

The CST considers appeals against decisions of the Chief Inspector of Schools in England and the National Assembly for Wales.

Carers UK

Carers UK (England)
20–25 Glasshouse Yard, London EC1A 4JT
Tel: 020 7490 8818
Fax: 020 7490 8824
Email: info@carersuk.org
Website: www.carersuk.org

Carers UK is a membership organisation established in 1965 and is the leading campaigning, policy and information organisation for carers in the UK.

Carers Scotland

91 Mitchell Street, Glasgow G1 3LN
Tel: 0141 221 9141
Email: info@carerscotland.org
Website: www.carerscotland.org

Carers Wales

River House, Ynsbridge Court, Gwaelod-y-Garth, Cardiff CF15 9SS.
Tel: 0292 081 1370
Email: info@carerswales.org
Website: www.carerswales.org

Carers Northern Ireland

58 Howard Street, Belfast BT1 6PJ
Tel: 0289 043 9843
Website: www.carersni.org
Email: info@carersni.demon.co.uk.

Chartwell's Child Trust

Hale Brook House, Scott Drive, Altrincham, Cheshire WA15 8AB
Tel: 0161 9293500
Email: info@childtrusts.co.uk
Website: www.childtrusts.co.uk

This is website provides information on the Child Trust Fund and explains how to maximise the investment.

Child Alert

64 Ellerby Street, London SW6 6EZ
Tel: 020 7384 1311
Email: info@childalert.co.uk
Website: www.childalert.co.uk

Childcare Alert offers advice, products and services relating to child safety in the community and at home.

Childcare Approval Scheme

2nd Floor, 23–25 Westbury House, Bridge Street, Pinner HA5 3HR
Tel: 0845 767 8111
Fax: 020 8866 7813
Website: www.childcareapprovalscheme.co.uk

This website provides information on the Childcare Approval Scheme, a voluntary scheme for carers who are not required to be registered by Ofsted.

Child Benefit Office

Tel: 0845 302 1444
Textphone: 0845 302 1474
Northern Ireland: 0845 603 2000
Northern Ireland Textphone: 0845 607 6078
If you live abroad: 0044 191 225 1000
Website: www.hmrc.gov.uk/childbenefit

The Child Benefit Office is responsible for the administration and payment of Child Benefit and Guardian's Allowance.

ChildcareLink

Tel: 0800 096 0296
Email: childcarelink@opps-links.org.uk
Website: www.childcarelink.gov.uk

The ChildcareLink national website provides childcare and Early Years information collected from English and Scottish local authorities, with information from the Welsh National Assembly. It also provides contact information of local **Children's Information Services** (CISs) in England and Wales, and of **Council Childcare Information Services** in Scotland.

The Children's Legal Centre

Wivenhoe Park, University of Essex, Colchester, Essex CO4 3SQ
Essex Children's Project Helpline: 01206 873 873
Education Law and Advocacy Unit: 01206 874 807
Email: clc@essex.ac.uk
Website: www.childrenslegalcentre.com

The Children's Legal Centre is a unique, independent national charity concerned with law and policy affecting children and young people. It provides legal advice and representation for children, their carers and professionals throughout the UK.

Child Support Agency

PO Box 55, Brierley Hill, West Midlands DY5 1YL
Helpline: 08457 133 133
Website: www.csa.gov.uk

The Child Support Agency is responsible for running the child support system. They assess, collect and pay child support maintenance.

Child Trust Fund

Waterview Park, Mandarin Way, Washington NE38 8QG
Tel: 0845 302 1470 (8am–8pm)
Welsh speakers: 0845 302 1489 (8.30am–5pm)
Textphone: 0845 366 7870
Email: childtrustfundoffice@ir.gsi.gov.uk
Website: www.childtrustfund.gov.uk

The Child Trust Fund is a government-sponsored organisation offering advice and information on Child Trust Fund and other child benefits.

Citizens Advice Bureau

National Association of Citizens Advice Bureaux, Myddelton House, 115–123 Pentonville Road, London N1 9LZ
Tel: 020 7833 2181 (only administration, not advice)
Fax: 020 7833 4371
Website: www.citizensadvice.org.uk
Information website: www.adviceguide.org.uk

The Citizens Advice Bureau (CAB) offers free advice to people on legal, financial and other problems, in over 3,200 locations. They also run and maintain an information website (see above) that provides useful advice on a number of issues including benefits, housing and employment, debt, consumer and legal issues.

Clybiau Plant Cymru Kids' Clubs

Tel: 029 2074 1000
Email: contact@clybiauplantcymru.org
Website: www.clybiauplantcymru.org

Clybiau Plant Cymru Kids' Clubs works in partnership with the Welsh
Assembly Government, the New Opportunities Fund, local authorities and
communities across Wales to develop out-of-school care.

Commission for Racial Equality (CRE)

St Dunstan's House, 201–211 Borough High Street, London SE1 1GZ
Tel: 020 7939 0000
Fax: 020 7939 0004
Email: info@cre.gov.uk
Website: www.cre.gov.uk

CRE works in both the public and private sectors to encourage fair
treatment and to promote equal opportunities for everyone, regardless of
their race, colour, nationality, or national or ethnic origin for a racially just
and integrated society, where diversity is valued.

CRE Scotland

The Tun, 12 Jackson's Entry off Holyrood Road, Edinburgh EH8 8PJ
Tel: 0131 524 2000
Textphone: 0131 524 2018
Fax: 0131 524 2001
Email: scotland@cre.gov.uk

CRE Wales

3rd Floor, Capital Tower, Greyfriars Road, Cardiff CF10 3AG
Tel: 02920 729 200
Fax 02920 729 220
Email: InformationWales@cre.gov.uk

Daycare Trust

21 St. George's Road, London SE1 6ES
Tel: 020 7840 3350
Fax: 020 7840 3355
Email: info@daycaretrust.org.uk
Website: www.daycaretrust.org.uk

This organisation is the national childcare charity, working to promote high quality childcare.

Department for Education and Skills (DfES)

Caxton House, Tothill Street, London SW1H 9NA
Tel: 0870 000 2288
Care to Learn helpline: 0845 600 2809
Email: info@dfes.gov.uk
Website: www.dfes.gov.uk

DfES is the government department responsible for education and skills.

Department for Work and Pensions (DWP)

The Adelphi, 1–11 John Adam Street, London WC2N 6HT
Tel: 020 7712 2171
Fax: 020 7712 2386
Website: www.dwp.gov.uk

DWP is the government department responsible for work and social security. It is responsible for Jobcentre Plus and the Disability and Carers Service.

Department of Health (DoH)

Richmond House, 79 Whitehall, London SW1A 2NL
Tel: 020 7210 4850
Minicom: 020 7210 5025
Email: dhmail@dh.gov.uk
Website: www.dh.gov.uk

DoH is the government department responsible for healthcare via the NHS and social services. Their website has information on Direct Payments.

Department of Health, Social Services and Public Safety (DHSSPS)

Caste Buildings, Stormont, Belfast BT4 3SJ
Tel: 028 90520500
Fax: 028 90520572
Email: webmaster@dhsspsni.gov.uk
Website: www.dhsspsni.gov.uk

DHSSPS administers the business of Health and Personal Services, Public Health, and Public Safety in Northern Ireland.

Department of Trade and Industry (DTI)

Response Centre, 1 Victoria Street, London SW1H 0ET
Tel: 020 7215 5000
Minicom: 020 7215 6740
Email: dti.enquiries@dti.gsi.gov.uk
Website: www.dti.gov.uk

DTI is the government department responsible for promoting business and industry and encouraging trade. The DTI's Employment Relations Directorate deals with relationships between workers and employers regarding both individual rights and collective agreements.

Directgov

Website: www.direct.gov.uk

Directgov is the web portal for government information and services.

Disability Alliance

Universal House, 88–94 Wentworth Street, London E1 7SA
Tel (voice and minicom): 020 7247 8776
Fax: 020 7247 8765
Email: office.da@dial.pipex.com
Website: www.disabilityalliance.org

The Disability Alliance provides free benefits advice for disabled people.

Disability Policy Division

Department for Work and Pensions, Level 6, Adelphi Building,
John Adams Street, London WC2N 6HT
Email: enquiry-disability@dwp.gsi.gov.uk
Website: www.disability.gov.uk

The Disability Policy Division is part of the Department for Work and
Pensions, and helps disabled people find out more about their rights and
learn about relevant legislation.

Disabled Parents Network

Unit F9, 89/93 Fonthill Road, London N4 3JH
Helpline: 08702 410 450
Text: 0800 018 9949
Email helpline: e-help@disabledparentsnetwork.org.uk
General enquiries Email: information@disabledparentsnetwork.org.uk.
Website: www.disabledparentsnetwork.org.uk

Disabled Parents Network (DPN) is a national organisation of and for
disabled people who are parents or who hope to become parents, and
their families, friends and supporters. It provides support, information,
advice and training for disabled parents.

Disabled Person's Tax Credit helpline

Helpline: 0845 605 5858
Textphone: 0845 608 88 44

Disability Rights Commission

DRC Helpline, FREEPOST MID02164, Stratford upon Avon CV37 9BR
Helpline: 08457 622 633
Textphone helpline: 08457 622 644
Fax: 08457 778 878
Website: www.drc-gb.org

The Disability Rights Commission (DRC) is an independent body established
to stop discrimination and promote equality of opportunity for disabled
people. It operates a helpline for enquiries regarding the Disability
Discrimination Act.

Dumfries Welfare Rights

50 Lincluden Shops, Dumfries, Scotland DG2 0QB
Tel: 01387 266888
Fax: 01387 263999
Website: www.welfarerights.net

Dumfries Welfare Rights aims to help educate people about their welfare rights, encourage the take up of benefit entitlements by providing information, and campaigning for improvements in provisions for the disabled, elderly and vulnerable.

Early Support Programme

Royal National Institute for Deaf People,
19–23 Featherstone Street, London EC1Y 8SL
Tel: 020 7296 8238 or 020 7296 8307
Website: www.earlysupport.org.uk

The Early Support Programme is a UK government initiative to improve services for disabled children under 3 years old and their families. It supports families and people working for education, health, social services and the voluntary sector.

Elizabeth Nuffield Educational Fund

The Nuffield Foundation, 28 Bedford Square, London WC1B 3JS
Tel: 020 7631 0566
Fax: 020 7323 4877
24hr answerphone: 020 7580 7434
Email: enef@nuffieldfoundation.org
Website: www.nuffieldfoundation.org

The Fund offers grants to support women studying to improve their employment prospects and commissions studies on the funding and caring needs of particular groups of women students.

Employers for Carers

Email: info@employersforcarers.org.uk
Web: www.carersuk.org/Employersforcarers

Employers for Carers is a partnership set up to identify and promote the business benefits of supporting carers in the workplace.

Employers for Childcare (Northern Ireland)

87 Main Street, Moira BT67 OLH
Tel: 028 9261 0661
Fax: 028 9261 0761
Email: info@employersforchildcare.org
Website: www.employersforchildcare.org

Employers For Childcare works with the business sector, government and childcare providers in Northern Ireland to promote family-friendly practices in the workplace. It offers advice on childcare, working entitlements and flexible working.

Equal Opportunities Commission (EOC)

36 Broadway, London SW1H 0BH
Tel: 020 7222 1110
Fax: 020 7222 2771
Email: info@eoc.org.uk
Website: www.eoc.org.uk

If you believe you have been unfairly treated at work or by anyone providing a service because of your gender, you can call the confidential helpline: 0845 601 5901

Scotland Office

St Stephens House, 279 Bath Street, Glasgow G2 4JL
Email: scotland@eoc.org.uk
Tel: 0845 601 5901
Fax: 0141 248 5834

Wales Office

Windsor House, Windsor Lane, Cardiff CF10 3GE
Email: wales@eoc.org.uk
Tel: 0845 601 5901
Fax: 029 2064 1079

The Equal Opportunities Commission is an independent, non-departmental public body, funded primarily by the government, working to eliminate sex discrimination. There is also an office in Manchester.

Faircare Services Ltd

1 Farnham Road, Guildford GU2 4RG
Tel: 0870 7770711
Fax: 01483 549100
Email: info@faircare.co.uk
Website: www.faircare.co.uk

Faircare Services is a provider of Childcare Voucher Schemes for employers.

Fathers Direct

Herald House, Lamb's Passage, Bunhill Row, London EC1Y 8TQ
Tel: 0845 634 1328
Email: mail@fathersdirect.com
Website: www.fathersdirect.com

Fathers Direct is the UK's national information centre on fatherhood. It provides news, training information, policy updates, research summaries and guides to support fathers and their families.

Foundation for People with Learning Disabilities (FPLD)

7th Floor, 83 Victoria Street, London SW1H 0HW
Tel: 020 7802 0300
Fax: 020 7803 1111
Email: fpld@fpld.org.uk
Website: www.learningdisabilities.org.uk

Scotland Office

Merchants House, 30 George Square, Glasgow G2 1EG
Tel: 0141 572 0125
Email: scotland@fpld.org.uk

FPLD promote the rights of people with learning disabilities and their families through research and projects.

Gingerbread

7 Sovereign Close, Sovereign Court, London E1W 2HW
Tel: 020 7488 9300
Advice Line: 0800 018 4318
Fax: 020 7488 9333
Email: office@gingerbread.org.uk
Website: www.gingerbread.org.uk

Gingerbread is the leading support organisation for lone-parent families in England and Wales.

Health and Safety Executive

Rose Court, 2 Southwark Bridge, London SE1 9HS
Tel: 020 7556 2100
Infoline: 0845 345 0055
Fax: 020 7556 2102
Website: www.hse.gov.uk

Britain's Health and Safety Commission (HSC) and the Health and Safety Executive (HSE) are responsible for the regulation of almost all the risks to health and safety arising from work in Britain. There are offices throughout the UK.

Home Dads

Tel: 07752 549085
Fax: 0870 132 7267
Email: info@homedad.org.uk
Website: www.homedad.org.uk

Home Dads is a UK support group dedicated to helping fathers at home with their children. Its website contains information, a forum for dads, and a chat room.

Jobcentre Plus Offices/local benefit offices

To find out the contact details of your local Jobcentre Plus, go to the **website** www.jobcentreplus.gov.uk

If you do not have access to the Internet, they are also listed in phone directories.

Learndirect

English helpline: 0800 100 900
Farsi: 08000 931 116
French: 08000 931 115
Gujarati: 08000 931 119
Polish: 08000 931 114
Punjabi: 08000 931 333
Somali: 08000 931 555
Sylheti: 08000 931 444
Urdu: 08000 931 118
Welsh: 0800 100 900
Typetalk: 0800 100 900
Minicom: 08000 568 865
Website: www.learndirect.co.uk

Learndirect is a Government backed e-learning initiative aiming to provide high quality post-16 education especially to those with few or no skills or qualifications. Learndirect has online learning centres in England, Wales, and Northern Ireland (but not Scotland).

National Children's Bureau (NCB)

8 Wakley Street, London EC1V 7QE.
Tel: 020 7843 6000
Fax: 020 7278 9152
Website: www.ncb.org.uk

NCB is an umbrella body for the children's sector in England and Northern Ireland, providing information on policy, research and best practice to their members and other partners.

National Child Minding Association of England and Wales (NCMA)

8 Masons Hill, Bromley, Kent BR2 9EY
Tel: 020 8290 8973
Fax: 020 8460 6157
Email: ncma.greaterlondon@ncma.org.uk
Website: www.ncma.org.uk

NCMA promotes and supports registered childminders in England and Wales by providing access to latest information, training and support. It can also help to advise parents on local accredited childminders.

National Day Nurseries Association (NDNA)

Oak House, Woodvale Road, Brighouse, West Yorkshire HD6 4AB
Tel: 0870 774 4244
Fax: 0870 774 4243
Email: info@ndna.org.uk
Website: www.ndna.org.uk

NDNA is the national membership association of day nurseries in the UK. It provides professional support, information and advice, and also runs training, seminars and conferences for professionals in the field.

National Debtline

The Arch, 48–52 Floodgate Street, Birmingham B5 5SL
Tel: 0808 808 4000
Website: www.nationaldebtline.co.uk

National Debtline provides free confidential advice on debt and useful factsheets.

The National Institute of Adult Continuing Education (NIACE)

Renaissance House, 20 Princess Road West, Leicester LE1 6TP
Tel: 0116 204 4200 or 0116 204 4201
Fax: 0116 285 4514
Email: enquiries@niace.org.uk
Website: www.niace.org.uk

Wales office

3rd Floor, 35 Cathedral Road, Cardiff CF11 9HB
Tel: 0292 0370900
Email: enquiries@niacedc.org.uk

NIACE is a non-governmental organisation that promotes adult continuing education in England and Wales.

National Lone Parent Helpline

Helpline for callers from Scotland: 0808 801 0323
Helpline for those south of the border: 0800 018 5026
Website: www.opfs.org.uk/aboutus/projects/helpline.html

The National Lone Parent Helpline offers advice to lone parents and is run by One Parent Families Scotland.

National Minimum Wage Enquiries

National Minimum Wage, Room 91A, Longbenton,
Newcastle upon Tyne NE98 1ZZ
Helpline: 0845 6000 678 (you can be assisted in 30 different languages)
Minicom: 0845 915 3296
Email: nmw@inlandrevenue.gov.uk
Website: www.inlandrevenue.gov.uk/nmw/nmw_help.htm

The helpline provides information about the national minimum wage.

National Parent Partnership Network (NPPN)

8 Wakely Street, London EC1V
Tel: 020 7843 6000
Website: www.parentpartnership.org.uk

The National Parent Partnership Network supports all parent partnership services across England. NPPN can provide contact information for your local parent partnership where you can get advice and support for parents of children with Special Educational Needs.

Nestor Healthcare Group

Beaconsfield Court, Beaconsfield Road, Hatfield, Hertfordshire AL10 8HU
Tel: 01707 255635
Fax: 01707 255633
Email: info@nestorplc.co.uk
Website: www.nestor-healthcare.co.uk

Nestor is an independent provider of personnel and service solutions to the health and social care market. Nestor provides the childcare approval service on behalf of the Government.

Northern Ireland Childminding Association (NICMA)

16/18 Mill Street, Newtownards, County Down BT23 4LU
Tel: 028 9181 1015
Fax: 028 9182 0921
Advice line: 02891 811015
Email: info@nicma.org
Website: www.nicma.org

NICMA is a charity and membership organisation working to support childminders, parents and children. It provides training and assessment for childminders; offers a Quality Assurance Scheme; provides a childminding information and advice service to childminders, parents and those involved in Early Years care; and provides a support network tor registered childminders.

Office for Standards on Education (Ofsted)

Headquarters address: Alexander House, 33 Kingsway, London WC2B 6SE
Tel: 020 7421 6800
Childcare helpline: 0845 601 4771
To complain about a childcare provider: 0845601 4772,
Website: www.ofsted.gov.uk

Ofsted is a non-ministerial government department responsible for inspecting educational standards in all schools and childcare provision, including childminders.

One Parent Families

One Parent Families, 255 Kentish Town Road, London NW5 2LX
Telephone: 020 7428 5400
Helpline: 0800 018 5026
Fax: 020 7482 4851
Email: info@oneparentfamilies.org.uk
Website: www.oneparentfamilies.org.uk

This organisation promotes supportive policies and services for lone parents and their children. It is a membership organisation, and also runs an advice service.

One Parent Families Scotland

13 Gayfield Square, Edinburgh EH1 3NX
Tel: 0131 556 3899
Helpline: 0800 018 5026
Fax: 0131 557 7899
Email: info@opfs.org.uk
Website: www.opfs.org.uk

This is a national voluntary organisation that promotes supportive policies and services for lone parents and their children. They have a telephone hotline on employment rights, benefits, maintenance, funding, and also offer training and counselling sessions.

Parents' Advice Centre (NI)

Floor 4, Franklin House, 12 Brunswick Street, Belfast BT2 7GE
Helpline: 0808 801 0722
Tel: (028) 9031 0891
Fax: (028) 9031 2475
Email: belfast@pachelp.org
Website: www.pachelp.org

The Parents' Advice Centre aims to promote positive parenting by providing support and counselling.

ParentsCentre

Website: www.parentscentre.gov.uk
ParentsCentre has been developed by the Department for Education and Skills as a resource to support parents. The website provides information for parents on how to help with their child's learning, including advice on choosing a school and finding childcare.

Parents for Inclusion

Unit 2, 70 South Lambeth Road, London SW8 1RL
Tel: 0800 652 3145
Email: info@parentsforinclusion.org
Website: www.parentsforinclusion.org

Parents for Inclusion is a national network of parents of disabled children. It runs a national helpline.

Parentline Plus

Tel: 020 7284 5500
Helpline: 0808 800 2222
Textphone: 0800 783 6783
Website: www.parentlineplus.org.uk

Parentline Plus is a national charity that offers advice to parents. Parentline Plus runs a helpline, and groups and workshops are run by the 12 local offices.

Pre-school Learning Alliance

Head Office address: The Fitzpatrick Building, 188 York Way, London N7 9AD
Tel: 020 7697 2500
Fax: 020 7700 0319
Email: info@pre-school.org.uk
Website: www.pre-school.org.uk

The Pre-school Learning Alliance represents and supports community pre-schools in England by offering support and advice.

Saving for Children

Elysium House, 126–128 New Kings Road, London SW6 4 LZ
Tel: 0845 606 6037
Website: www.savingforchildren.co.uk

Saving for Children offers advice to parents to help them prepare for the financial costs of children.

Scottish Childminding Association

Suite 3, 7 Melville Terrace, Stirling FK8 2ND
Tel: 01786 445377
Advice Line: 01786 449063
Website: www.childminding.org

The Scottish Childminding Association (SCMA) is a support and information organisation in Scotland for registered childminding. It also provides information for employers and parents.

Scottish Commission for the Regulation of Care (The Care Commission)

Compass House, 11 Riverside Drive, Dundee, DD1 4NY
Tel: 01382 207 100
Helpline: 0845 603 0890
Website: www.carecommission.com

The Care Commission regulates care services in Scotland on an annual basis.

Scottish Out of School Care Network

Level 2, 100 Wellington Street, Glasgow G2 6DH
Tel: 0141 564 1284
Fax: 0141 564 1286
Email: info@soscn.org
Website: www.soscn.org

The Scottish Out of School Care Network is a Scottish charity that promotes, supports and develops good quality, sustainable out-of-school care.

Scottish Pre-School Play Association

45 Finnieston Street, Glasgow G3 8JU
Tel: 0141 2214148
Fax: 0141 221 6043
Website: www.sppa.org.uk

Scottish Pre-school Play Association supports children and families in Scotland through the development of quality early education and childcare services.

Sector Skills Development Agency

3 Callflex Business Park, Golden Smithies Lane, Wath-upon-Dearne, South Yorkshire S63 7ER
Tel: 01709 765444
Email: info@ssda.org.uk
Website: www.ssda.org.uk

The Sector Skills Development Agency (SSDA) funds, supports and champions the UK-wide network of employer-led Sector Skills Councils (SSCs). SSCs are employer-led, independent organisations that cover a specific sector across the UK. They provide employers with a forum to express the skills and productivity needs of their sector.

Special Educational Needs and Disability Tribunal (SENDIST)

London office (address for disability discrimination claims):
Procession House, 55 Ludgate Hill, London EC4M 7JW
Darlington office (address for SEN appeals): Ground Floor, Mowden Hall, Staindrop Road, Darlington DL3 9BG
Tel: London – 020 7029 9726, Darlington – 01325 391045
Helpline: 0870 241 2555
Email: tribunalqueries@sendist.gsi.gov.uk
Website: www.sendist.gov.uk

Parents whose children have special educational needs can appeal to SENDIST against decisions made by local education authorities (LEAs) in England and Wales about their children's education. SENDIST provides advice for parents on tribunals and is independent of both central and local government.

Stonewall

46 Grosvenor Gardens, London SW1W 0EB
Tel: 020 7881 9440
Fax: 020 7881 9444
Minicom: 020 7881 9996
Email: info@stonewall.org.uk
Website: www.stonewall.org.uk

Stonewall is a charity group that works to ensure that the rights and needs of lesbians, gay men and bisexuals are addressed.

Sure Start

Sure Start Unit, Department for Education and Skills and Department for Work and Pensions, Level 2, Caxton House, Tothill Street, London SW1H 9NA
Tel: 0870 0002288
Email: info.surestart@dfes.gsi.gov.uk
Website: www.surestart.gov.uk

Sure Start is the Government's programme to deliver the best start in life for every child by bringing together early education, childcare, health and family support. The Sure Start Unit has responsibility for a wide range of universal programmes, as well as those targeted on particular local areas or disadvantaged groups within England.

Tax and Benefits Confidential Helpline

Helpline: 0845 608 6000

The Tax and Benefits Confidential Helpline offers advice and help for people doing "cash in hand" work who want to get their tax and national insurance affairs in order.

Tax Credits Helpline

Helpline: 0845 300 3900
Textphone: 0845 608 6000
Northern Ireland Helpline: 0845 603 2000
Northern Ireland Textphone: 0845 607 6078
Website: www.taxcredits.inlandrevenue.gov.uk

The Tax Credits Helpline will enable you to apply for Tax Credits, alert the Inland Revenue to a change in your circumstances and provide help with filling in the form.

TeacherNet

Tel: 0870 000 2288
Fax: 01928 794 248
Email: info@dfes.gsi.gov.uk
Website: www.teachernet.gov.uk

TeacherNet is a website run by the Department for Education and Skills aiming to help education professionals find the information they need quickly and easily.

Tiger (Tailored Interactive Guidance on Employment Rights)

Website: www.direct.gov.uk/Employment/Employees/fs/en

Tiger is a government website providing information on different aspects of UK Employment Law, including adoption, employment, maternity and paternity rights, Flexible Working and the National Minimum Wage.

Tommy's, the baby charity

Nicholas House, 3 Laurence Pountney Hill, London EC4R 0BB
Tel: 08707 70 70 70
Pregnancy information line: 0870 777 30 60
Fax: 08707 70 70 75
Email: mailbox@tommys.org
Website: www.tommys.org

Tommy's is a UK charity dedicated to maximising health in pregnancy.

UK Database of Women Experts in SET

WiTEC UK, c/o Inova Consultancy, 45A Crescent Road, Sheffield S7 1HL
Tel: 01298 85134
Fax: 0114 2207127
Email: info@setwomenexpertsuk.org.uk
Website: www.setwomenexperts.org.uk

This searchable database contains information on women who are considered experts within their field of Science Engineering and Technology occupations. The tool aims to raise awareness about the skills and knowledge of women in the field.

Women and Equality Unit

1 Victoria Street, London SW1H 0ET
Tel: 020 7215 5000
Minicom: 020 7215 6740
Website: www.womenandequalityunit.gov.uk

The Ministers for Women, supported by the Women and Equality Unit (WEU), are responsible for promoting and realising the benefits of diversity in the economy and more widely, including balancing work and family life.

Working Families

1–3 Berry Street, London EC1V 0AA
Tel: 020 7253 6253
Fax: 020 7253 6253
Email: office@workingfamilies.org.uk
Website: www.workingfamilies.org.uk

Working Families offers advice and information to employers, families and carers about working and childcare.

Women Returner's Network (WRN)

Website: www.women-returners.co.uk

WRN is an organisation dedicated to helping women returners achieve their aspirations.

INDEX

16 hour rule	143-6, 160
30 hour rule	68, 144, 159
4 Children	235
4 Nations Child Policy Network	235

A

Accor Services UK	235
Action for Blind People	236
Additional Maternity Leave	11, 21-2
Adoption	9, 47-56
Adoption Leave and Pay	9, 47-56
Adult and Community Learning (ACL)	11
Adult Learning Grant (ALG)	11, 218-9
Advisory Centre for Education (ACE)	236
Advisory, Conciliation and Arbitration Service (ACAS)	11, 236
Alternative employment	20
Annual Leave	23, 61, 73
Annualised hours	67
Antenatal care	20-1, 37, 43
Apprenticeship	215-6
Armed forces	37, 41, 59, 69, 169
Association for Women in Science and Engineering (AwiSE)	237
Attendance Allowance	11
Au Pair	97-9

B

Basic Skills	211-2
BBC Parenting	237
Biological father	38, 41
Breastfeeding	76-8
British Au Pair Agencies Association (BAPAA)	237
Business and Technology Education Council	11
Business Case	70-1
Business Link	237

C

Care Standards Directorate	86
Care Standards Inspectorate for Wales (CSIW)	238
Care to Learn	222-3

Career break	67
Career Development Loan	219-20
Careers Scotland	227
Careers Wales	227
Carer's Allowance	11
Carers	65, 151, 160, 189
Carers Northern Ireland	239
Carers Scotland	238
Carers UK	238
Carers Wales	239
Chartwell's Child Trust	239
Child Alert	239
Child Benefit	12
Child Benefit Office	240
Child Element	141
Child Support Agency	241
Child Tax Credit	140-3
Child Trust Fund	166-175
Childcare	79-136, 222-4
Childcare Approval Scheme	239
Childcare Link	106
Childcare Options	79-193
Childcare Support	218
Childcare Vouchers	161-5
Childminder	118-122
Children's Centres	132
Children's Legal Centre	240
Children's' Information Service	134
Citizens Advice Bureau	241
Civil Partnership	7
Clybiau Plant Cymru Kid's Clubs	242
Commission for Racial Equality (CRE)	242
Company Car	23, 61, 182
Compassionate Leave	73
Compressed working hours	67
Compulsory Maternity Leave	21
Confidence Building	198-203
Connexions	228-9
Contact a Family	135
Contribution-based benefits	185-7
Council Tax Benefits	158-60
CRE Scotland	242

CRE Wales   242
Crossroads   136

D

Daily nannies   91
Dance and Drama Award   221
Day Nursery   112-4
Daycare Trust   243
Department for Education and Skills (DfES)   243
Department for Trade and Industry   244
Department for Work and Pensions (DWP)   243
Department of Health (DoH)   243
Department of Health, Social Services and Public Safety (DHSSPS)   244
Department of Trade and Industry (DTI)   244
Dependent children   150
Detained in hospital   189
Directgov   244
Disability Alliance   244
Disability Living Allowance   141, 145
Disability Policy Division   245
Disability Rights Commission   245
Disabled Child Element   141
Disabled children   127-136
Disabled Parents Network   245
Disabled Persons' Tax Credits   63, 245
Disadvantage Test   145
Dismissal   31, 52
Divorce   189
Dumfries Welfare Rights   246

E

Early Support Programme   246
Education Maintenance Allowance   223-4
Elizabeth Nuffield Educational Fund   246
Emergency Leave   74-5
Employers for Carers   246
Employers for Childcare   247
Enterprise Nursery Scheme, The   191-3
Equal Opportunities Commission (EOC)   247
Evaluating a job   208
Experience   200

F

Faircare Services Ltd.	148
Family Element	141
Fathers Direct	248
Financial Support for Learning	218-24
Flexible Working Appeal Form	10
Flexible Working Application	10
Formal Leave	10, 70-1
Foundation for People with Learning Disabilities (FPLD)	248
Free Part-time Early Learning	83
Free School Meals	143
Funeral grants	143
Further Education	229

G

Gingerbread	249
Grandparents	58
Guardian's allowance	188-90

H

Health and Safety Assessment	18-20
Health and Safety Executive	249
Health and Social Services Trust	86-7
Health benefits	143
Health Club Membership	23, 61
Her Majesty's Revenue and Customs	141
Higher Education	229
Home Dads	249
Housing Benefit	158-60

I

Illness	28
Incapacity Benefit	185
Income Support	62-3
Income Tax	155-7
Independent Schools Council Information Service	116
Informal Leave	73
Intensive Activity Period	232-3
International Au Pair Association	99
Internet	207

J

Job adverts	205
Job grades	212-3
Job Share	68
Jobcentre Plus	228
Judiciary	37-41

K

Kids Clubs	122-6

L

Learndirect	213, 226
Learner Support Fund	220-1
Learning for free	213
Live-in nannies	90-1
Low skills	211

M

Manual Skills	202
Matching certificate	49, 54
Maternity Allowance	28-30, 186
Maternity Certificate	18
Maternity Leave and Pay	16-35
Maternity Pay Period	24

N

Nanny	90-6
Nanny agencies	94
Nanny-share arrangements	91
National Childbirth Trust	94
National Childminding Association	121
National Children's Bureau (NCB)	250
National Day Nurseries Association (NDNA)	251
National Debtline	251
National Instituted of Adult Continuing Education (NIACE)	251
National Insurance	151
National Lone Parent Helpline	252
National Minimum Wage Enquiries	252
National Parent Partnership Network (NPPN)	252
National Qualifications Framework	211-3
National Vocational Qualification	213
Nestor Healthcare Group	253
New Deal for Lone Parents	233-4

Nextstep providers	227
Northern Ireland Childminding Association (NICMA)	253
Notice period	32-3
Nursery Class	110-7

O

Official Notification	55
Ofsted	86-7
One Parent Families	254
Open University	216
Ordinary Maternity Leave	17, 21
Out of home childcare	100-26
Out of School Care	122-6
Overpayments	148

P

Parent and Toddler Group	106-7
Parent Partnership Services	133
Parent Support Groups	135
Parental Leave	57-63
Parental Leave Scheme	62
Parental responsibility	8
Parentcraft Classes	20
Parentline Plus	255
Parents Advice Centre	254
ParentsCentre	255
Parents for Inclusion	255
Part time	17, 59, 68
Partner	7
Passive smoking	19
Paternity Leave and Pay	36-45
Pension	23, 183, 186
People Skills	201-2
Playgroup	107-110
Police force	41, 75
Pregnancy-related illness	28
Premature	27
Pre-retirement	68
Pre-school Learning Alliance	255
Prescriptions	143, 157
Prison	146, 189, 211
Professional Association of Nursery Nurses	96
Professional journals	205

Q

Qualifications	209-216
Qualifications and Curriculum Authority	215

R

Reasonable provisions	76
Recruitment and Employment Confederation	94, 99
Redundancy	21, 23, 32, 51
Reference books	205
References	105
Registered Childcare	85-7
Relaxation classes	20
Resignation	31
Rest facilities	77
Returning to Education and Training	195-234
Returning to work	31-5, 51

S

Sabbatical	68
Salary Sacrifice	182-7
Same-sex partner	7
Saving for Children	256
Savings Accounts	171
Scottish Childminding Association	256
Scottish Commission for the Regulation of Care (The Care Commission	256
Scottish Out of School Care Network	256
Scottish Pre-school Play Association	257
Sector Skills Development Agency	257
Self-certificate	49, 53, 54
Self-rostering	68
Severely Disabled Child Element	141
Shares	171
Shift working	68-9
Sick Pay	30, 186
Skills	200-2
Special Educational Needs	210-6
Special Educational Needs and Disability Tribunal (SENDIST)	257
Special Leave	69
Staff discount	22-3, 51
Stakeholder	171
Statutory Adoption Pay	54
Statutory Maternity Pay	24-7, 186,

Statutory Paternity Pay	40-5
Statutory Sick Pay	186
Stillborn	22, 38, 44
Stonewall	258
Study Leave	69
Sure Start	132, 258
Sure Start Maternity Grant	177-80

T

Tax and Benefits Confidential Helpline	258
Tax Credits	139-48
Tax Credits Helpline	259
TeacherNet	259
TEDS Management	192
Temporary work	207
Term-time working	69
Tiger (Tailored Interactive Guidance on Employment Rights)	259
Tommy's, the baby charity	259
Twins	59, 152

U

UK Database of Women Experts in SET	260
Unfair dismissal	52
University and Colleges Admissions Service	229
Unregistered Childcare	85-6

V

V-time working	69

W

Women and Equality Unit	260
Women Returners' Network	203, 207
Work experience	207
Working Conditions	19-20, 77
Working Flexibly	64-75
Working Hours	21, 32, 54, 65-9, 73
Working Tax Credit	143-6
Workplace Nurseries	112, 192
Young children	32, 65, 132